CW01335713

TEN POUND POMS

Our Journey to a New World 'down under'

Sandra Burdett

authorHOUSE®

AuthorHouse™ UK Ltd.
1663 Liberty Drive
Bloomington, IN 47403 USA
www.authorhouse.co.uk
Phone: 0800.197.4150

Published by AuthorHouse   11/14/2013

ISBN: 978-1-4918-7801-9 (sc)
ISBN: 978-1-4918-8324-2 (e)

With love to our daughter Sue, who continues our Australian dream, and in loving memory of our son Rodney, who is such a large part of our story.

Contents

Acknowledgements ix

Prologue xi

1   How it all began 1
2   Making plans.................................... 9
3   Honeymoon in Jersey 21
4   Ship Ahoy! 29
5   Foreign shores 35
6   All at sea 43
7   Stormy waters.................................. 49
8   Settling in (Perth)............................. 55
9   Looking for work (Perth)...................... 63
10 Earthquake! 71
11 Fun and games................................ 77
12 Melbourne here we come! 85
13 Employment in Melbourne 95
14 Out and about in Melbourne 105
15 Trip to Sydney 115
16 Special Visitor 125
17 Fun times in Melbourne & Victoria........... 133
18 New arrival 141
19 Joy and sorrow................................ 149
20 Work and play 159
21 Trips to England and Scotland 167
22 Home visits 175
23 A home of our own............................ 185
24 Wedding bells 193

25 Avon calling! 201
26 A special gift 209
27 Pain and suffering 221
28 Difficult decisions 231
29 Return journey 241

Epilogue 247

Acknowledgements

I am very grateful to family and friends in England and Australia for their help with names, dates, places and editing. Thanks also to Geoff for his constant support and patience.

Prologue

During the years 1945-72 around one million migrants were encouraged to depart the British Isles for a new life 'down under' in Australia, with promises of a better lifestyle, increased job prospects, decent housing and of course, fabulous weather!

The cost of the fare at the time, once accepted as a migrant, was just £10 (ten pounds sterling) per adult, with children travelling free. This fare was subsidised by the Australian Immigration Service, whose minister created the so-called 'Ten Pound Pom' scheme, firstly to increase the population of Australia, and secondly to provide much-needed workers for the booming industries which included textiles, building and agriculture, but especially engineering and mining.

The word 'Pom' I believe, is defined as 'Prisoner of His/Her Majesty'—a reminder that the majority of the first settlers, as opposed to the indigenous Aboriginals, were British convicts sent our on ships to serve long sentences, working on the land or in service, sometimes for petty crimes. Many died on the long hazardous journey, but others served their time and were then free to live and work in Australia, but few earned enough for their return fare home.

During the post-war years migrants departed for Australia not just from the United Kingdom, but also from the Republic of Ireland, Malta and Cyprus, and in later years from Italy, Greece, West Germany and Turkey. Thankfully the experience was very different from that of those original settlers, but it was still a brave move to leave everything familiar behind to face an unknown future.

Our own adventure began in December 1967, when we boarded the *Fairstar* liner in Southampton to begin our new life on the other side of the world.

1

How it all began

"There's one!" I shouted. Our hire car drew to a halt at the kerbside, next to the bright red Royal Mail postbox and Geoff, my new husband of just one hour, in his smart navy suit with white carnation in the buttonhole, leapt out and posted a very special letter into its gaping mouth. This was addressed to *Australia House*, London and contained the final paperwork required for our application to emigrate to Australia, including our new marriage licence—with the ink hardly dry!

Wedding day, 16th September 1967

The date was 16th September 1967 and we were on our way from the church to our wedding reception. We had been accepted as migrants, passed our medicals and had our travel papers ready, but the Australian High Commission would not give us a date to travel until we had provided the last document required—proof of our marriage. Things were very 'moral' in those days! We then continued our journey to enjoy a party with family and friends, before flying off on our honeymoon to *Jersey* in the *Channel Islands*.

This followed more than three years of planning. About a year after we met and began dating ('courting' it was called in those days), Geoff talked about Australia, and how great it would be to live and work there. When he was quite young his mother had talked about the possibility of moving to Australia, but unfortunately circumstances did not allow this at the time. One day Geoff said he would really like to emigrate and asked how I felt about it. I remember saying it would be fine for a man to face that journey and future alone, but a young woman would need the security of marriage to embark on such a big adventure. His reply? "Well, will you?" I said "Yes" immediately and that was that—no formal proposal—no ring, just an agreement between us, and an understanding that in the not-too-distant future we would embark together on a journey to the other side of the world! I had learnt about Australia at school in geography lessons, but never dreamt that one day I would be considering living there.

We didn't think of ourselves as formally engaged at that time, but were in love, and happily looking forward to a future life 'down under' in Australia, 12,000 miles away from family and friends, but full of exciting opportunities. We didn't mention any of this to our families then—after all, I was only 16 and Geoff 19, so we were content to keep it to ourselves and to make plans, without anyone dampening our enthusiasm by expressing doubts as to the wisdom of such a big undertaking. To us it was exciting, and we set out to learn as much as we could in the meantime about this new country we were planning to make our own.

Geoff was born in Leicester General Hospital on 10th February 1945, and I was born there just over three years later on 29th February 1948. I was a 'breech baby'—"feet first", my mother said—and strangely she always reminded me of this every time I needed a new pair of shoes! I had two older sisters, Pat and Sylvia, who evidently used to tease me when my birthday was due—as I was a 'Leap Year' baby, and 29th February came around just once every four years, they would say on non-Leap Years that it wasn't my birthday on 28th February, but the day after—1st March—that I had missed it! They were only joking of course, and my birthday was celebrated every year. It does mean though, that I have aged very slowly!

Geoff and I met in May 1963 on our local park when I was a schoolgirl of 15 and he was an 'older man' of 18. I was living in a rented terraced house at No 8 *Crystal Street* with my divorced mum, Margaret (known as 'Maggie' when we were young) and two older sisters, Pat and Sylvia, and Geoff lived in a rented council property with his grandparents, Kate and Josh, two unmarried uncles, Ken and George, and his brother, 'young' Ken. Geoff and his older brother had lost their mum to cancer when she was 38 and they were just 14 and 17, and as their mum was also divorced, their grandma gave them a loving home. She enjoyed nothing more than feeding up her family of men, and did so right to the end of her life aged 83.

I often went to nearby *Abbey Park* after school, sometimes with a friend, Barbara, and sometimes with our next-door neighbours' two children, who I took care of after school until their parents came home from work. This public park covers 57 acres and contains the remains of *Leicester Abbey,* built in 1143 and demolished by King Henry VIII in 1538, and also part of *Cavendish House*, built from the old materials and used by Charles I after the siege of Leicester in 1645. The king's soldiers set fire to it after he left, leaving it gutted. *Cardinal Wolsey* died at the Abbey in 1530 while on his way from York to London. There is a memorial to him in the Abbey ruins and a statue outside the Park café. The *River Soar* runs through the centre of the Park, and on the east side is a boating lake, bandstand, bowling greens, rose gardens and a model railway. On the other side of the river, as well as the Abbey ruins, is a café, the Oval, where cricket is played in the summer, tennis courts and a pet's corner for the children. There is also a recreation area with swings, slides and, at that time, a shallow concrete paddling pool. (The paddling pool is still there, but sadly not filled with water these days). This was where young people in the area would congregate in the evenings and on week-ends—with many of us having no gardens, we treated this as our very own 'back yard'.

Geoff visited the Park quite often with his friend, Colin and we chatted—luckily I had changed out of my school uniform, so he didn't know how young I was! I tried flirting with him, but couldn't have been very good at it, because it took ages for him to ask me out. Even then, it took another lad to ask me out for Geoff to step in and say, "She's coming out with me". Result! We walked back in a group to the end of my street and arranged to meet the next evening. Then after a quick good-night kiss, I went home to find something to wear for that special first date, and Geoff went off to the pub with his mates.

Nearly three years later, on Christmas Eve 1965, we became officially engaged, with a diamond and sapphire ring for me, a plain gold band for Geoff (he didn't want a 'fancy' ring) and a party for family and friends at 32 *Stephenson Drive*, a council property my mum, sister Sylvia and I had moved into the year before. This was a huge improvement on the house in *Crystal Street*, as it had an in-door water supply and a bathroom—luxury! My sister Pat had moved into her own house after marrying Ted two years before, and now had a son Anthony (Tony), my beloved nephew—I was so thrilled to be an aunty! Geoff and his family lived at 52 *Stephenson Drive*, so it was just a short walk for them to come and celebrate with us. Geoff's brother had married two years before and he and his wife Ann and their children, Diane and 'little' Geoff also joined us.

We had a lovely celebration and have fond memories of that night, when a group of carol singers came to the door to serenade us. After one verse each of "Away in a Manger" and "Good King Wenceslas" and a quick burst of "We Wish You a Merry Christmas", we invited them inside for sausage rolls and mince pies, and to hand over a small collection of coins to share. There were four boys, and the smallest of them insisted that they should divide up the spoils before they left, as he was afraid he wouldn't get his fair share once they were back on the street!

2

Making plans

Now that we were formally engaged we could get down to the serious business of planning our future. We needed to save hard for our wedding, and we also started filling in the paperwork for our application to emigrate to Australia. We opened a joint bank account at our local TSB branch and Geoff retrieved his bankbook from the safe hands of his grandmother, who had cared for it since he was at school. I don't think I contributed much to this account at the time, but we started as we meant to continue, sharing everything equally, as we have done ever since.

On Geoff's Honda 250 Dream

Geoff made the supreme sacrifice—he sold his beloved motorbike, a *Honda 250 Dream*. He had been paying this off in instalments, so this money could now go into the kitty. It had been our only mode of transport, so it was back to buses and 'Shanks's pony'—walking! We did miss the bike, as we'd had some good trips on it, dressed in our leather jackets and wearing matching crash (safety) helmets. The weather wasn't always kind to us though, and I remember one particular Easter week-end trip to *Great Yarmouth* in *Norfolk*. We had met the rest of Geoff's family there and stayed overnight—I slept in a caravan with Geoff's grandma (and the dog!), and Geoff shared with his granddad and two uncles. The return journey was horrendous—it was cold, with rain lashing down, when the zip on Geoff's leather jacket broke. We swapped jackets as he was getting the brunt of the harsh winds, and I squeezed up behind him as closely as I could. With hail and sleet stinging our faces, we eventually made it back to Leicester, after many hours. Geoff dropped me off at No 32 and I walked stiffly to the door. My hands were so cold I couldn't get my key into the lock on the front door, and had to ask a bemused young boy passing by to open the door for me. Geoff had carried on to No 52, and he just dropped the bike under the window outside the house before going inside to thaw out.

I had been working in an office since leaving King Richard III Intermediate School, and was attending evening classes in the same building to learn shorthand and typing. I'm afraid I gave up the shorthand classes, as three evenings a week studying were a bit much after full-time work and I did want to see something of Geoff! Office work was very poorly paid at the time and on hearing from friends that good money could be earned in the many knitwear firms in Leicester, I applied to be a cutter at *Kemptons*, a firm manufacturing sweaters and dresses, and was duly set on. At that time everyone employed in producing these garments—knitters, cutters, overlockers and finishers, were paid at a set rate per dozen items, known as 'piecework'. After a shaky start, I was soon earning a good weekly wage. It was non-stop, repetitive work, but my fellow workers were friendly. I shared a cutting table with Janette, and we sang along to 'Workers Playtime' on the radio. I remember particular hits at the time were "Please Release Me" by Engelbert Humperdinck—a Leicester lad—which seemed to be played every hour and "There's a New World Somewhere they call the Promised Land" by the Seekers, which seemed appropriate as we were planning our own trip to a 'New World'.

Cutters at the time were using open electric circular blades, with a metal protector in the opposite hand, which held the work steady. In my early days as a novice cutter I quite often forgot to use the guard, much to the dismay of my fellow workers, who couldn't say anything at the time, as they were afraid they would distract me and cause an accident. Needless to say it was a dangerous practice, and one day I managed to slice off a small area of the tip of my left index finger. I was rushed up two flights of stairs to the nurse, who promptly stuck my profusely bleeding finger into hot, salty water! This harsh treatment seemed to work and my finger healed with no lasting effects, but I had certainly learnt my lesson! I worked for two years in the cutting section at *Kemptons,* with a brief spell in the sample/design department. I was put on a good set wage here, but there wasn't much work and the time dragged, so I asked to go back to the cutting room, with it's hustle and bustle and camaraderie. It was back to piece-work again though, and sometimes I questioned my decision when we were short of work and put on part-time hours.

Geoff had a good job as a sample knitter at *Byford*'s, manufacturers of socks and knitwear, so we began saving hard for our wedding and future. We still enjoyed our Monday nights at the cinema (our first date had been a trip to the *Odeon*, though I can't remember which film we saw). We also paid a weekly visit to the *Fish and*

Quart, a *Berni Inn*, where we would have a steak meal or plaice and chips (fries). Geoff would have a beer, and I would have a schooner of port—we certainly knew how to live! Another popular dish in pubs at the time was 'chicken in a basket'—a wicker basket filled with chips and half a chicken. The only fast-food outlets in those days were fish and chip shops and *Wimpy* burger bars—how times have changed!

We had seen advertisements in newspapers written by the Australian government, who were recruiting all over the country for people willing to move to Australia to live and work—"Come to sunny Australia for £10!" Members of the Migration Service attended meetings in pubs and clubs to give talks, advice and film shows to interested parties. Geoff and I attended weekly meetings at *The Barley Mow* pub in Granby Street, along with around twenty other like-minded people. Most were young, some with small children, but all had the same purpose— to find out if emigration to Australia was the right path for them. The information given covered all the capital cities of each state, *Perth* in Western Australia, *Adelaide* in South Australia, *Melbourne* in Victoria, *Sydney* in New South Wales, *Brisbane* in Queensland, *Darwin* in the Northern Territory and *Hobart* in Tasmania. The talks covered jobs, housing, living costs, education, and also the choice of either flying to Australia (24 hours travel time) or sailing (a month). Geoff and I didn't need much convincing. We decided that *Perth* in Western Australia would be our destination, and we jumped at the chance of a four-week cruise. I think the Australian Immigration Service would have preferred everyone to fly, but we couldn't be persuaded otherwise, even with the threat of being allocated different cabins on board the ship! It was explained to us that although our assisted passages would only cost us £10 each, we would have to pay for our own private health checks and any costs of travel/identity documents and travel to the airport or ship. All food would be provided on the plane or ship, but alcoholic drinks (duty free) would be extra. In our own case, as 'sailors', expenses incurred on our two excursions to *Las Palmas* in the *Canary Islands* and *Cape Town* in *South Africa* would also fall to us. We couldn't wait to start our journey!

During this time we were also planning our wedding. In the sixties most couples married in either March or September, as these were the best times of the year for tax purposes—either in tax refunds or no tax payable for a few weeks after marriage—a great start to wedded bliss! We decided to tie the knot in September 1967, so off we went to see Reverend Yeomans, the vicar of our local church, St Augustine's. Because the majority of weddings were in March or September, venues for receptions were booked up early, so we needed to arrange a date for the wedding itself as early as possible. Rev Yeomans was very understanding, and even though we were not regular church attendees, we had both been Christened—Geoff by the Salvation Army, mainly to take advantage of the day trips to the sea-side—he agreed to marry us on 16th September 1967 at 12 noon. He took our details—names, addresses and ages, and entered them into his diary. Our ages at the time were 18 and 21, and a year later the details on our marriage certificate stated the same, so we can always claim to be a year younger than we actually are—though I've never been sure if this error means we are not legally married, and have been 'living in sin' ever since!

We went away feeling pleased that our plans were coming together, but half-way home realised we hadn't paid our account. We went straight back to the rectory, which was only a couple of streets away, and knocked on the door. Reverend Yeomans came to the door in his pyjamas and dressing gown—I think the poor man had been planning an early night!

The next thing to organise was our wedding reception. As we were paying for this ourselves and had only a small budget, we looked around for something affordable—castles and manor houses were definitely out, so a pub seemed a good option. We made enquiries at several locations and finally settled on a pub we had frequented with friends, which was fairly close— *The Leicestershire Yeoman.* (This later became *The Last Straw* and is now a *Kentucky Fried Chicken* takeaway!) We booked an afternoon buffet for around forty family and friends and paid a deposit. So the two most important things were arranged, and we still had a whole year to finalise the minor details.

That year passed quickly as we sorted out such things as invitations, transport, gifts— for each other and for our bridesmaids, a photographer to record the happy event, a new suit for Geoff, and of course, my wedding dress. I also wanted to lose some weight—don't all brides want to look their best on their special day? This wasn't too difficult, as working full-time and rushing from shops to photographers and for dress fittings left little time for eating. My sister Pat, who worked as a dressmaker, was making my wedding dress and the dresses for my bridesmaids. She also made herself a smart suit to wear, all this on top of having a new baby daughter, Sharan, who was only three weeks old on our wedding day. We have a lovely photo of me in my wedding dress holding my baby niece, which set some tongues wagging!

After trying on a few ready-made dresses in bridalwear shops to decide on a style (cheeky!), Pat and I had a lovely time looking for patterns for my dress and for the bridesmaids' dresses. We found suitable patterns in *Lewis*'s store in Leicester city centre, but no fabrics that appealed, so we decided on a day trip to *Nottingham* to search out material and, of course, some world-famous *Nottingham lace*. *Nottingham* was only a half-hour train journey away, so we had a few hours to shop to our hearts' content. We scoured many *Nottingham* stores and, with a brief stop for lunch, managed to cover quite a distance in our search for the perfect items. We were very pleased with our final purchases; white satin and lace for my floor-length gown and long train, pale gold satin and lace for the bridesmaids' dresses, and we even found some cream wool for Pat's suit, my treat to her for making our dresses. All-in-all it had been a very successful day out.

My nephew Tony was to be our 'page boy', and we hired the cutest little suit for him to wear— shiny black trousers, white satin shirt with black bow-tie, and black patent leather shoes with silver buckles. He was only three years old at the time though and didn't appreciate the importance of the occasion. I remember throughout the church service hearing little sobs coming from the front pew, and thinking it was my mum getting sentimental about losing her youngest daughter, when actually it was my little nephew, who told his mum afterwards: "You shouldn't have let me be a pageboy"!

Geoff and I went shopping for my wedding ring. I chose a plain gold band, but Geoff didn't need another ring as he had been wearing a plain gold one since our engagement. His wedding gift to me was a gold cross and chain, and I bought him a gold tie pin. For our bridesmaids— my cousin Peggy-Jane aged 12 and Geoff's two cousins, Lynda 14 and Tricia 6—we bought single pearls on gold chains. We also visited my Uncle Tom, one of my mum's brothers, to ask if he would 'give me away', which I think really pleased him as he and Aunt Stella had no children of their own. They were a big part of our childhood, taking my sisters and me on trips to the seaside, and we loved visiting them in their house in *Conduit Street.* Their back garden wall overlooked *Leicester Railway Station*, and we three urchins loved to sit on this to watch the steam trains set off to faraway places such as *London* (getting very dirty faces from the soot), but more exciting to us were the trains making their way to the seaside towns of *Mablethorpe* and *Skegness* in Lincolnshire.

We were also lucky to have mum's sisters to visit. Aunt Kath (Kathleen) and Uncle Lol

(Lawrence) lived close by with our cousins, Iris and Jean, and we spent many special Christmas Days with them. They lived within walking distance, and I can remember one Christmas Day walking home in the dark after enjoying lovely food and party games with the snow falling all around—a very special time. Mum's eldest sister, Rose, lived in Coalville with Uncle Fred, and our cousins Derek, Paddy and Marian. We loved to catch a big red double-decker bus to go to Coalville, thinking it was so far away, when actually it was only 12 miles, and sometimes we would stay overnight.

Things were coming together nicely, and we were still compiling as much information as we could about Australia. Our excitement mounted the nearer the time came to our wedding and possible early departure to the Antipodes. We had one more thing to plan—our honeymoon. As we would be staying with my mum after our marriage until we received a date to sail for Australia, we thought we should have at least a week away on our own to begin married life. A friend of Geoff's at work talked about a holiday she and her family had recently had in *Jersey* in the *Channel Islands*, and we decided this would be perfect—just a short flight away, leaving from *East Midlands Airport*, and the weather in September promising to be warmer than the

British Isles. We booked seven nights in bed and breakfast accommodation in *St Helier*, close to the beach. It was a very exciting time, with so much to look forward to, and we were eager for the next chapter in our life together to begin.

3

Honeymoon in Jersey

After we had posted our very special letter our driver, Brian, drove us, the happy bride and groom, to our wedding reception, where our family and friends were waiting to celebrate with us. We had hired a coach to take our guests without cars from the church to the pub and intended the bridesmaids to travel with them, but somehow they were left behind, and poor Brian had to make an extra journey back to the church to collect them, where they were anxiously waiting in the September drizzle. I've heard that if it rains on your wedding day you will be rich, so I suppose a slight drizzle is better than nothing!

The celebrations in the pub went very well, and the 3-piece band we had hired (three young lads—a drummer, a guitarist and a singer) played our favourite songs—anything by *The Beatles*, *The Rolling Stones* or *Motown*! Geoff gave a short speech thanking everyone for their kind wishes and gifts, some of which were of cash, as everyone there knew we would be travelling to Australia shortly and would have limited luggage allowance. Before we knew it, the time had come for me to change before we had to leave to catch our flight. My 'going-away' outfit was a smart blue *lurex* dress and coat, which elicited a very cheeky comment from a male friend! We left everyone in the capable (or not, depending how much he'd had to drink!) hands of the Best Man, Ken, and Brian arrived to collect us for our trip to *East Midlands Airport*. Everyone came outside to throw more confetti and to see us on our way. I threw my wedding bouquet, which was caught by a young work colleague—I'm not sure if she was the next to wed. There was much kissing and shaking of hands. Geoff, who had drunk quite a few beers and the odd spirit or two and was in a merry mood, kissed all the ladies and shook hands with the men, including Brian, who said, "I'm taking you to the airport, mate!" It was lovely to settle into the back of the car, relax and talk about our day, as it seemed like I had hardly seen or spoken to Geoff over the last few hours—even when the photos were being taken outside the church, he kept disappearing to chat to friends!

We arrived at the airport in plenty of time for our 7pm flight to *Jersey*. While waiting to be called to board the plane we tried not to look like newly-weds, but with me in my shiny outfit and Geoff in his smart suit, shirt and tie, I don't think we fooled anyone! *Jersey* was a very popular honeymoon destination at that time, and we weren't the only self-conscious young couple in the airport lounge sipping coffee while waiting for their trip to paradise! The air hostess did tell us later that they called this particular Saturday evening flight "The Honeymoon Special"!

Neither Geoff nor I had flown before, but it was a smooth flight. The plane was small, a propellor-driven DC9 and the flight was of only 75 minutes duration, so by the time we had been served tea and biscuits and chatted about our wonderful day, the plane touched down in *Jersey*. It was a lovely warm evening—quite a change from the dampness we had left behind. We took a taxi to the bungalow in which we had booked our accommodation for the coming week. Our host made us very welcome. He showed us to our room at the front of the house. The bay window had lovely views of the well-kept neighbouring gardens, still very colourful in this temperate climate. He handed Geoff the keys to the front door and our room and suggested we might like to take a walk along the beach before retiring. He pointed us in the right direction, and as tired as we were after our special day, we did enjoy the short walk to the shore and the fresh sea breezes. After months of planning and a hectic but wonderful wedding day, we were really looking forward to our future together as husband and wife.

Jersey is a wonderful island, the largest of the *Channel Islands*, situated in the *English Channel* just twelve miles from the coast of *Normandy* in *France*. It is approximately forty miles round, and we were keen to see as much of it as we could during our week there. On our second day we were walking around *St Helier* and Geoff spotted a car hire shop. He didn't have a car driving licence at the time, but saw some motorbikes at the back of the store which were also for hire. He arranged to rent a black *Honda CB125* for the next few days and took out his wallet to pay. To his embarrassment, confetti fluttered onto the counter! The salesman just smiled and, with flushed faces, we climbed onto the bike and rode away. The motorbike was the perfect way to explore the island. Geoff is an early riser, and the next morning he left before breakfast to enjoy a solo ride right around the island. I breakfasted alone, thinking this might be the shortest marriage ever, but he returned really happy, so how could I complain?

We also booked some excursions during our stay, one of which was a dinner and dance. We were there with another two couples we had met previously in a pub—Sid and Wynne, who were in their forties, and a younger couple in their twenties, whose names I'm afraid escape me. One of them had requested the band to play 'The

Anniversary Waltz' for us because we were newly married, but Geoff and I were too embarrassed to take to the floor, especially as we weren't expert at ballroom dancing—'twisting' was more our scene. The floor gradually filled up with other couples, but I do wish now we'd had the courage to get up and dance to that special song. We also had a lovely day on the beach with our new friends playing football and swimming, but sadly didn't keep in touch with them after our return to England and subsequent journey to Australia.

Two wonderful places to visit on the island of *Jersey* are the *Jersey Pottery* and *Jersey Pearl*. The Pottery was established in 1946 and has been a family-run business since 1954. It is a world-renowned centre for ceramics, with excellent restaurants, and sells the most wonderful tableware, homeware and gifts. My particular favourites were the table lamps, especially in bold colours of blues, reds, oranges and yellows— colours echoed in the pretty surrounding gardens. I was very tempted to purchase one of these wonderful lamps, but of course it would have been far too delicate to withstand the trip back to England, and then on to Australia.

Jersey Pearl was established on the island 25 years ago and is a spectacular showroom for pearls from around the world, set in sparkling silver and gold. I could have spent a day there in this fabulous setting, with the light bouncing off glass cases of necklaces, earrings, watches and rings—the latter being a particular weakness of mine! Of course such small items would have been very transportable, but we couldn't afford anything at the time. However, we did return to *Jersey* on our 25th Wedding Anniversary and made another trip to *Jersey Pearl*, when I was able to treat myself and several work colleagues to some special drop pearls to be hung on gold or silver chains.

One place we didn't visit on our honeymoon, but did take a tour round on our Silver Anniversary trip, was the infamous *Underground Hospital*, built by prisoners during the time of German occupation in World War II. These slave labourers were mostly Russian, Polish, French and Spanish. The hospital was quite a feat of engineering, designed by Germans but blasted and hewn out of the rocks by forced labour. It was meant as an underground fortress for the German occupiers and was built on a slope for natural drainage, with the incorporation of air-conditioning and central heating. There was an operating theatre, wards, offices and connecting tunnels. On our tour we were horrified to learn of the harsh treatment of these prisoners. Interestingly, during our visit in 1992 there were quite a few Germans in the group being led through the tunnels by a tour guide and at first there was much loud talking, but as we progressed further and gained more information of the inhumane treatment of these prisoners, it became much quieter, as all nationalities realised the true horror endured by thousands of workers, many of whom died from disease, malnutrition, accidents and exhaustion. We did understand that the Germans visiting then were possibly researching their own family history, and were probably as shocked as us by what we witnessed.

Our wonderful week in *Jersey* was coming to an end so we returned the motorbike to the hire firm, packed our bags and took a taxi to the airport. We were soon winging our way back to reality. On arrival at *East Midlands Airport* we boarded a coach to transport us back to Leicester, a journey of less than an hour, and as the coach pulled into *St Margaret*'s Bus Station, we saw our local bus about to depart. Geoff grabbed our bags and we ran to catch it. He sorted the change in his pocket and all he had left was four pence—exactly the right fare of two pence each! What a relief to get home—happy but penniless!

4

Ship Ahoy!

Once back home in Leicester we settled down to work and to wait impatiently for that all-important letter which would give us our date to sail off to our new life in Australia. I remember waiting at a bus stop at the end of *Stephenson Drive* on a cold, dark and rainy November evening wishing we could be in Australia's warm, sunny climate, and being able to discard the many layers of clothes we had on to keep out the cold.

Within a week the letter had arrived—we were to set sail on 3rd December from Southampton on the ship *Fairstar*. We were so excited and couldn't wait to tell our family and friends—I don't think they had believed we would really go until then. Most seemed pleased for us, even though my sister Pat had said "But you're terrified of spiders!" (I never did get over that fear). She was also sad that we wouldn't be there for Christmas—we would be celebrating this on board our floating temporary home. There were some negative comments, such as "You'll be back", but overall I think the majority were happy for us, and perhaps a little envious.

We had less than two months to wait now and the days flew by. We packed all our worldly goods into two 24" square by 36" tall packing cases— just large enough to contain some precious framed photographs, our wedding album, some bedding, clothes and small engagement and wedding gifts. It didn't look like much, but we thought it would be enough to give us a start in our new life—the rest we were sure we could purchase once we had settled into a flat in Perth—though at the time we had no idea what sort of accommodation we would find on arrival. We were very naïve, I suppose, because all the advertising and promises made by the Australian Immigration Service concentrated on the positive aspects, such as finding work easily and the abundance of new homes just waiting to be purchased. The reality was quite different, but we were lucky to be without a house to sell or children to take out of school and away from their friends. I know that sometimes families with older children found the move caused much upheaval and resentment. As it was we were young, newly-married and ready for adventure.

On 2nd December 1967, we took a taxi to *Leicester Railway Station* to begin our epic journey. Two other cars with mine and Geoff's families aboard followed, and we all piled onto platform 3 to wait for the train to London, where we would transfer to the 'boat train' to *Southampton*. We had a while to wait and we spent most of the time chasing after Geoff's nephew, "little Geoff", who was running about the platform, getting very close to the edge to inspect the tracks! My sister now had two children, Tony and Sharan, and Geoff's brother had a daughter, Diane, son, Geoff, and their new baby girl, Marie, and we were sad to think of missing them growing up. Of course, as most migrants did, we thought we would see them in a year or so when they came over for a holiday in the sunshine. Unfortunately the fare was quite prohibitive for families, and it is when your children are young with perhaps only one parent working, that you can least afford expensive trips. However, we were looking forward to having our own family in the future, and hopefully trips 'home' to introduce our little Aussies to their English family.

We arrived at *St Pancras Station*, *London* in the late afternoon and found our way through the throng to the 'boat' train for *Southampton*. With hardly a break we were on our way. The train arrived in the evening and we needed to find a bed for the night before boarding our ship the next day. As we waited outside the station in the rain for a taxi, we saw a group of blue and white-clad football supporters—they were *Leicester City Football* fans, who had travelled to *Southampton* to cheer on their team. Geoff was surprised to see them and especially pleased to hear that the 'Blue Army' had won the game!

We hadn't thought of booking any overnight accommodation in advance, which was probably unwise, given that there was a ship leaving from Southampton the next day—with approximately 1200 passengers plus crew. We mentioned to the taxi driver that we needed to find a bed for that night, and he used his radio to contact a few people he knew who offered bed and breakfast amenities. After several failures, he took pity on us and drove us to his home—much to the surprise of his wife! She did occasionally cater for travellers needing bed and breakfast, and though it was short notice, she was very welcoming. We felt ourselves very lucky to find such kind people, who had taken us in at a moment's notice. We had a lovely night's sleep—even with the prospect of the next day looming and our journey into the unknown. Our friendly taxi driver said to me at breakfast-time, "I can tell your husband slept well—I could hear him snoring"! After our substantial full English breakfast, he took us and our luggage to the port, and wished us well for the future.

In front of us loomed a beautiful all-white and shiny ocean-going liner. At 24,000 tons, the *Fairstar* was perhaps smaller than many of today's luxurious cruise ships, but it looked very impressive to us against the pale blue winter sky—even the sun was out to wish us 'bon voyage'! Unfortunately we didn't get to walk up the gang-way to board the ship as, after leaving our suitcases to be transferred, we walked up a flight of stairs, and then along a walkway which led directly onto the ship. There were crowds of people, but the crew were very efficient, and kept us all moving along smoothly. We were directed to what would be our accommodation for the next four weeks and, as predicted by immigration officials, we were to sleep in different cabins. Only eleven weeks married, and already to be separated! The cabins were on a lower deck and central, with no portholes. Fortunately ours were next to each other. They were very compact, with four bunk beds, two up and two down, and a very small toilet and shower room. I was to share with three other young married women, and Geoff was next door sleeping with their husbands! I am happy to say that during the voyage we did manage quite a few intimate moments back in one of the cabins, as did our shipmates—helped by having different mealtimes! At least we didn't have to resort to a lifeboat, which many loving couples did. On such a crowded ship it was often hard to find much-needed privacy.

We returned to the outer deck, where most passengers were gathering to wave goodbye to friends and relatives on shore. Coloured streamers were being thrown from ship to shore, for loved ones to cling to as a last link to all that was familiar before the final separation. As there was still about an hour before our ship was due to set sail, and on the advice of someone we took to be a seasoned traveller, we went 'below' to the huge dining room, where we joined a long queue to reserve our seats for mealtimes and to decide on first or second sittings for dinner. It took so long to sort this out that when we eventually returned to the deck, the ship had already set sail. The broken streamers were hanging lifelessly over the rails, and we could see the white cliffs of Dover fading in the distance. Our long journey had begun!

5

Foreign shores

Our ship, the *Fairstar*, was converted from a troopship (the Oxfordshire) in 1964, and was based in Sydney, Australia. It was used almost exclusively for migrant voyages until 1974, when it became a cruise ship, sailing to and from Sydney and the South Pacific. It was one of four ships of the *Sitmar Line*, the others being the *Fairsky*, *Fairsea* and *Castel Felice*. Its maiden voyage was in May 1964, sailing from Southampton to Sydney, full of British migrants. It carried almost 2,000 passengers plus crew, on a 'One Class Tourist' basis, which was still the same during our voyage in 1967. There was nowhere on this 'floating hotel' that we didn't have access to, though young children were banned from some of the bars.

Apart from our rather cramped sleeping quarters, facilities aboard the *Fairstar* were equivalent to a 4-star hotel. The two restaurants were excellent, providing the most amazing dishes, with self-service breakfast, buffet-style lunch, and waiter service 4-course dinners, with two sittings at 6pm and 8pm. The crew were mostly Italian, and naturally there was much flirting with the female passengers, greatly enjoyed by the single girls, but inevitably leading to several altercations between crew and some husbands—one involving the purser and a policeman!

There were two swimming pools, the deeper of which swimmers could dive into and wave through a round window to people drinking in the lounge on a lower deck. Many activities were organised around the pools, one particularly memorable one was that of celebrating the crossing of the equator. The crew put on fancy dress, and first-timers across the 'line' were thrown into the pool—we managed to avoid that indignity. Everyone was presented with a certificate to mark this special occasion. It did seem strange though that on our crossing the weather was hot, but the rain poured down, and the crepe paper decorations worn by the revellers stained everyone all the colours of the rainbow.

The *Promenade Deck* had deck-chairs arranged for those inclined to relax and maybe read, and on the *Boat Deck* was the *Lido Bar* near to the swimming pool. The *Sunset Lounge*, *Aquarius Lounge and Night Club*, and the *Zodiac Lounge and Bar* catered for all tastes, and there was even a cinema in the bowels of the ship—one of the films we saw was 'Blue Hawaii' with Elvis Presley, which certainly put us in the mood for warmer climes! Also down on a lower level was a laundry with washing machines and driers. This was always busy with so many passengers aboard. It was the only chore we had to undertake ourselves—no cooking, dish-washing or bed-making—so we couldn't complain! It was a good place to chat with other passengers too, such as mothers with young children whom we might not meet in the lounges and bars, and to hear of their histories and hopes for their futures in Australia. There was even a hairdressing salon on board, and quite a few men took advantage of the chance to get a trim. The trouble was, no matter what style each man requested, they all came out sporting a crewcut! Geoff had booked himself an appointment before we realised this—but his crewcut quite suited him and was the ideal style for the warmer weather. Our 'floating hotel' seemed to be equipped with everything we could possibly need over the forthcoming days and weeks, and we intended to make the most of it!

Our cabin-mates, who we came to know very well over the voyage, were all British. Barbara and Roy were in their late twenties and from Leeds—Roy was a painter and decorator and Barbara an office worker. Anne and Tommy were in their mid-twenties and had met in London, but were originally from Yorkshire and Glasgow. Geoff and I, at 19 and 22, were the babies of the group! The fourth couple sharing our cabins were from London. We cannot recall their names, but we do remember them telling us about some of the contents of their luggage—especially the whips and knives! We weren't sure what they used these for (we hadn't heard of S & M then), but we couldn't wait to see what the Australian customs officials would make of them! The six of us enjoyed exploring the ship together and took full advantage of all the amenities, especially the duty-free drinks! After late-night drinking sessions we would often be too late for breakfast, so we would head for the *Jungle Room* for coffee and pastries. This was situated above the *Captain's Bridge* and gave us unrestricted views over the bow of the ship, looking over the vast ocean to the distant horizon. After three days of sailing we were looking forward to stepping ashore at our first port of call, *Las Palmas* in the *Canary Islands*.

The usual route for ships sailing to Australia at that time was via the *Suez Canal*, which links the *Mediterranean Sea* to the *Red Sea*. Completed in 1869, it is approximately 100 miles long, and is the fastest crossing from the *Atlantic Ocean* to the *Indian Ocean*, so ideal for trade between Europe and Asia. Liners and cruise ships use it constantly too, but in 1967 the *Canal* was closed to shipping by Egypt during the *Arab-Israeli War*, which followed many years of turmoil and disputes, especially the nationalisation of the

Canal in 1956 by President Nasser of Egypt. The result of this latest conflict was that foreign ships were denied access to the *Suez Canal* and had to undertake the much longer journey south through the *Atlantic Ocean* and around Africa, and, in our case, across the *Indian Ocean* to Australia.

The *Fairstar* docked in *Las Palmas* in the early morning with the temperature already over 70°F. The *Canary Islands* are situated just off *North Africa* and they enjoy a Mediterranean climate. It was early December, and so lovely to be able to spend a day sightseeing without coats (or umbrellas). In the dawn light we could see lines of taxis on the dockside, with the drivers vying for our custom as hundreds of passengers disembarked, anxious to make the most of their day ashore. The *Canary Islands*' population is mostly Spanish, and the drivers shouted to us in Spanish and English to attract our attention. Barbara, Roy, Anne, Tommy, Geoff and I walked along the dock, and enquired of the first driver we encountered how much the fare would be into town. "Only queeeds", he said. The first quote being too high, we kept walking until the last available taxi cost us just two pounds! Luckily they accepted pounds sterling, as non of us had any pesetas.

The town centre was just coming alive as we arrived, with noisy markets, and shops displaying the brightest colours of blankets, pottery and leather goods. We had much fun trying on sombreros and ponchos. I purchased some pretty tie-dyed fabric, our friends bought some gifts and souvenirs, and we continued our exploration of the town. Unfortunately it was very hard to shake off the local sellers, who would not take 'no' for an answer, and we were pursued along the streets by persistent youngsters waving their wares above their heads. One young lad of about 12 even pinched my bottom to get my attention! Quite a different shopping experience from any local High Street in Britain, but fun all the same. We had our first taste of Spanish food, paella, and brightly-coloured fish dishes—quite a change from our usual cod and chips.

In the afternoon we spent some time on the beach, and before heading back to the ship the boys became desperate to find a public toilet. Not knowing the Spanish for this, they tried the only word they could think of "hombre". The local man they asked looked puzzled and in the end Geoff had to demonstrate by unzipping his jeans—but going no further. Luckily the Spaniard understood and pointed them in the right direction, much to their relief. Time was getting on and we needed to get back to our ship. We saw a bus heading for the dock area and had to make a quick dash to catch it. Geoff was the last to use the local facilities, and saw us all boarding the bus. It started to move off and he made a spurt and leapt aboard, banging his knee quite hard on the upright grab rail as he did so. He could feel the blood running down his leg, but didn't get any first aid until we were back on the ship. He still has a scar on his knee to remind him of that day. We arrived back at the dock at dusk, and the *Fairstar*'s lights were shining from all the decks and portholes, seeming to be welcoming us home.

6

All at sea

The next leg of our journey continued south on the *Atlantic Ocean*, along the west coast of Africa, towards the *Cape of Good Hope*, arriving at *Cape Town*, *South Africa* ten days later. We had been told to expect some rough weather, but, I am happy to say, it was smooth sailing all the way. We continued to explore 'our' ship and fell into a routine of leisure activities such as swimming and deck quoits, and also joined in some organised games in the lounges. It was the first time I had played Scrabble, which I still enjoy today. There was entertainment every evening in the bars and night club, including fancy dress evenings. It was after sailing a few days along the coast of Africa that we crossed the equator and had the ceremony of 'crossing the line', as described in Chapter 4.

Although most people aboard were assisted migrants, there were some fare-paying passengers too. Some of these were Australians returning home, and one day on deck Geoff met a recently-retired couple returning to Melbourne, Mr & Mrs Calwell. Arthur Calwell had been in politics and was Leader of the Opposition (Labour) from 1960 to 1967. He and Geoff got on well and had some interesting conversations. Arthur gave Geoff some good advice, such as investing money in a plot of land as soon as possible, rather than buying expensive cars and going on trips. We valued this advice, and did actually act on it soon after arriving in Perth.

On 17th December there was some shocking news which travelled around the ship like wildfire. The Australian Prime Minister, Harold Holt, was lost at sea while swimming off Cheviot Beach in Victoria and presumed drowned. He had been in Australian politics for many years, but only became Prime Minister in 1966, and served just 22 months. His body was never recovered, and though there were some conspiracy theories at the time—usual in political circles—the most likely reality was that he drowned or was taken by a shark. We found it quite ironic later to learn that a swimming pool in Melbourne had been named 'The Harold Holt Memorial Pool'!

Much as we were enjoying our extended holiday afloat, with restaurant meals every evening followed by drinks and entertainment in the bars and club, we couldn't wait for our next excursion ashore. This was to be one full day in *Cape Town*—a once-in-a-lifetime experience. We docked in the early morning as before, to give us as many hours as possible to explore this beautiful city.

We took a single-decker bus into the town centre, where we had our first experience of apartheid. The seats were labelled 'white only' and 'black only'—the seats at the rear being for black Africans. We had never experienced anything like this and were very shocked. I almost took a stand by sitting on the 'blacks only' seats, but thought better of it, as I didn't want to disrupt our group's limited time ashore. It was very unsettling though, and gave us all something to think about. Geoff encountered another racial episode later that day, when he went into a local shop for a newspaper. There were three black men in front of him waiting to be served, but the white shopkeeper looked over their heads and asked "Can I help you, sir?" Geoff was embarrassed, but it was taken as the norm by everyone else in the shop. Looking back now, I realise it wasn't so different at that time to Australia's 'White Australia Policy', under which we were emigrating. We had much to learn about the treatment of aboriginals in Australia too.

We bought a picnic lunch and the six of us walked through the lovely city gardens, where we were delighted to see the cutest little chipmunks running about, much like the squirrels in Britain, but much friendlier, taking pieces of bread from our hands.

Geoff and I and our four friends had planned ahead to join other passengers on a recommended trip to the top of *Table Mountain*, which looms majestically over *Cape Town*. The mountain towers over 3,700 feet, and the peak can be reached by cable car. The first 1,000 feet is undertaken by energetic hikers, or for the less mobile, by bus. We joined the others at the bus station to begin our journey. This proved to be a nail-biting experience up the mountain on winding roads. It was almost a relief to climb aboard the swinging cable car to be transported to the highest point. Each car carried up to 25 people, and we six intrepid explorers climbed into a swaying cabin for an unforgettable experience. The 'cars' had huge windows which gave 360-degree views over *Cape Town* and the magnificent mountain. Even Geoff, who is not keen on heights, appreciated that this was really the only way to fully appreciate the aspects of *Cape Town* below us and *Table Mountain* above.

Geoff on Table Mountain, overlooking Cape Town

We reached the flat top of the mountain and joined the other tourists admiring the wonderful views over *Cape Town* and *Table Bay*. It was much cooler up there too, about 70°F, compared with almost 90°F in the town. We had a leisurely lunch in the mountaintop restaurant, and after three weeks of four-star dining aboard the *Fairstar*, most of us settled for plain chicken and chips—delicious! We all enjoyed a tall glass of ice-cold fresh milk too—which was no longer available on the ship after so many days at sea. Our journey back down the mountain was a bit more eventful. There had been an accident on the mountain involving climbers, and a rescue helicopter flew *under* our cable car to give assistance. Geoff was holding on very tightly to the safety bars of the car at this stage! The trip in the bus back to the base of the mountain was even scarier too, at what seemed inappropriate speed for the conditions, and I think we all closed our eyes and prayed for a safe outcome! After we had stopped shaking though, we all agreed it had been one of the best experiences of our lives.

So, it was back to our now familiar 'lodgings', and another ten days sailing, this time through some very stormy seas. We also had Christmas celebrations to look forward to, before our final destination, the port of *Fremantle* in *Western Australia*.

7

Stormy waters

We settled back into our routine aboard ship, but by this time it seemed a lot smaller and restricted—we felt 'hemmed in' with not being able to get away from other passengers for some much-needed solitude. We knew it wouldn't be long now though before we could spread our wings, so were determined to make the most of the last days of our voyage. Unfortunately the unpredictable weather wasn't going to let us have it all our own way. Soon after we had set sail from *Cape Town*, there were severe storms, which lasted three days. Passengers were suffering terrible bouts of seasickness, and the decks were awash. The ship's doctor was kept busy treating the desperately ill, with many patients confined to their cabins. Our group managed to avoid this 'mal de mer', and we tried to keep on deck as much as possible to breathe in the fresh, but very wild, air. We had to cling onto the handrails tightly when moving around the ship, and we could hear piles of plates and dishes smashing in the galley. The broken crockery wasn't missed, as the restaurant was almost empty at mealtimes during those turbulent days! During the nights in our dark cabin I strapped myself into my top bunk (straps were provided for just such a purpose), and clung onto the side of my bed as the ship rolled from side to side.

Eventually the sea became calm once again and we had a period of smooth sailing across the *Indian Ocean,* with warm temperatures and blue skies. This didn't last long, as without warning (for us at least), our ship was enveloped in white, clinging fog. It wasn't cold, but very eerie and quiet. The ship was cocooned in this strange, silent world for another few days. She (I felt I could call her that now, after such a long acquaintance) never slowed in speed at all, sailing silently onwards—thank goodness for radar!

Christmas was fast approaching, and once we had sailed through the fog we could again enjoy the experience of our 'half-way-round-the-world' cruise. The weather was hot and sunny, and we topped up our tans on deck during the day. In the evenings Geoff and I would take romantic walks on deck, watching the reflection of the moon on the calm sea. As before, it was the calm before the storm. All around us passengers were now succumbing to a stomach bug. The medical staff were once more working to full capacity, administering pills and potions. Again, our small group was lucky to escape this latest catastrophe.

The ship was decorated with bright lights along the decks, and Christmas trees in the bars and lounges. Santa even managed to visit the children—I think he must have come down the ship's funnel! Christmas services were held, and seasonal hymns and carols were broadcast over the ship's tannoy system—though "I'm Dreaming of a White Christmas" hardly seemed appropriate! On Christmas Eve we gathered in the *Aquarius Lounge* for some wonderful seasonal entertainment. Our friend Roy didn't join us though, as he was feeling quite ill, with 'flu-like symptoms. He had to stay in the cabin and was given an injection in a very delicate part of his anatomy!

Christmas day dawned bright, warm and sunny with calm seas. We had some small presents to open from family and from each other, and then went up for breakfast. Unfortunately Geoff was now feeling very under the weather, with the same symptoms as Roy. He returned to the men's cabin, and medical assistance was requested. Roy was still confined to the cabin, and both men's eyes lit up when a very attractive blonde nurse came to visit. Geoff's face soon changed when she took out a large syringe and told him to turn over and roll down his pyjamas! He has never forgotten the pain of that injection! Roy, who was now feeling a lot better, thought it was hilarious. Thankfully they both made a quick recovery.

This all meant that I had to go for the evening Christmas dinner without Geoff, though there were others sharing our table. I put on my little black dress and entered the restaurant. "Ah, Miss Fairstar!" exclaimed the waiter. It cheered me up, but of course I knew he said the same to many other young women. It did make his tip at the end of the voyage quite a bit bigger though! He noticed Geoff's absence, and asked where he was. His English wasn't too good and my Italian practically non-existent, but I tried to explain that Geoff wasn't well. He pointed to his stomach, but I indicated 'no' and pointed to my head—I don't know what he made of that! The dinner was delicious as usual, typically English, but with some additional Italian touches. I met our friends in the bar afterwards for a drink, but retired early to my lonely top bunk, separated by just a thin wall from my new hubby—so near yet so far!

Our last three days on board the *Fairstar* were spent shopping for last-minute souvenirs and duty-free drinks, packing our cases and swapping addresses. Our new friends were disembarking in *Fremantle* too, along with a few hundred others, with the rest of the passengers having a short break before travelling on to *Adelaide, Melbourne, Sydney* or *Brisbane*. Before we knew it, we were pulling into the port of *Fremantle*.

Everywhere there was hustle and bustle—on the ship and on shore. Geoff, Roy and Barbara were looking over the rails, and Barbara exclaimed "Look, men in shorts and long socks!" It was a strange sight to us—even on the ship on the hottest days there was hardly a man to be seen in shorts. The Australians on shore did look smart though, with short-sleeved shirts, ties, shorts, long socks and tie-up shoes. We later found this to be the usual summer attire for workers in offices and banks in *Fremantle* and *Perth*. At last we walked down the gangplank onto Australian soil after 25 days at sea. We had finally reached our destination—it was now up to us to make the best future for ourselves that we could in this country full of opportunities, we believed, for those not afraid to work hard and take chances.

It felt very strange walking on solid ground after weeks at sea. We had developed our 'sea legs' while on board ship, and now had to adjust to land which wasn't moving beneath our feet. All the passengers were walking with a very strange rolling gait as we assembled to be processed through passport and customs control. Geoff and I had no problems with our small amount of luggage and few souvenirs, but as we passed through we saw our London friends from aboard ship. The contents of their suitcases and boxes were spread out over several tables, and some very bemused and somewhat suspicious customs officials were giving them the third degree about the 'arsenal' they were bringing into the country!

We emerged from the custom shed into bright sunshine. The temperature was already around 85 degrees in the shade, but luckily our sea voyage had helped us to acclimatise to the heat. There were crowds outside waiting to meet families and friends, and some employers waiting to collect those lucky migrants who had jobs and accommodation waiting for them. We heard our names called and were met by a uniformed driver, who was to take us to a hotel in *Perth* for our first night's stay. The car was a black limousine, flying an Australian flag. We felt so special sitting in the back of this luxurious car, and enjoyed our first views of our newly-adopted country on the 12-mile drive to *Perth*.

It was late afternoon when we arrived at the *King's Park Hotel* in *Perth*. After checking in we took a short walk along *St George's Terrace*, the business centre of the city, before returning to our hotel, hot and tired, and looking forward to our first night's sleep ashore—together. The friendly manager wished us "Good-night", and asked us what we would like for breakfast—bacon and eggs—or steak and tomatoes? Now we really knew we had arrived in 'the land of plenty'!

8

Settling in (Perth)

Perth, the capital of *Western Australia*, was founded in 1829 along the *Swan River*. In the late 19th century the population increased substantially after the discovery of gold, with most of the influx being prospectors from the eastern states. There were also increases in population after World War II, and in later years due to mining operations, including iron ore and the discovery of natural gas. By the time we arrived in 1967 the population had swelled to over 700,000. Situated at the south-west corner of Australia, *Perth* was once said to be the most remote city in the world, but it is argued that *Honolulu* or *Auckland* in *New Zealand* may have that honour. Our first impressions were of a city of wide, clean streets, filled with sun-tanned people on their way to work in cool, air-conditioned shops and offices. There was not much industry in Perth itself, and many workers would travel to the oilfields for months at a time. The work in these remote areas was very hard, but well-paid.

Our hotel was situated close to *King's Park*— an area of 400 hectares (988 acres) of parkland, bushland and botanical gardens overlooking *Perth*. It is a very popular recreation area for city dwellers, with walks and picnic areas, and is also a good source of education for schoolchildren (and adult newcomers) to learn about the natural flora and fauna of their homeland, and of its history. Its elevated height gives wonderful views over *Perth* and the *Swan River*. We were really looking forward to exploring this national park as soon as we were settled.

On our first morning, after a very different but delicious Aussie breakfast, we set out to explore our new surroundings. The temperature was already close to 100°F, the sun was shining, the sky was blue, and there was a heat haze as we looked along *St George's Terrace* into the distance. Our first priority was to call into the State Bank to see if our money had been transferred from our bank in Leicester. Unfortunately, just before we left Britain the pound had been devalued, and we saw quite a difference in our finances when our pounds sterling were changed into Australian dollars. This new currency took some getting used to after pounds, shillings and pence, and for a few weeks we were changing every purchase back into sterling in our heads to calculate the cost. This became exhausting, and we eventually settled into the much easier decimal currency.

Our next urgent task was to find ourselves some accommodation. We were responsible for paying for our room at the hotel and on seeing the cost per night, knew we had to find somewhere cheaper quickly or our savings wouldn't last long. Geoff asked the very friendly staff at the bank if they knew of any flats that might be vacant. A young bank clerk said she thought there might be something available in a block of flats in *Adelaide Terrace,* which leads directly on from *St George's Terrace*, and which would be very convenient for us. We thanked her and caught a tram outside the bank—another novelty for us—and travelled the short distance. The tram driver dropped us off (in the middle of the road) opposite *The Causeway Flats*, and we went directly to the office at the front of the red-brick, six-storey block, through the car park. On enquiry the manageress told us that unfortunately all the flats were taken. On seeing our crestfallen faces though, she said there was a flat above the office on the first floor, but that it wasn't usually rented out. She agreed to show it to us however, and we followed her to the rear of the flats, which were built in two U-shaped blocks, one facing towards *Adelaide Terrace*, and one facing towards the *Swan River,* just 200 yards away at the rear. The access was via a courtyard, up some stone steps and along a verandah at the back.

The flat had an oblong lounge with a window to the front, a tiny kitchen with gas cooker, and a small bedroom, also facing to the front, with a bathroom/en suite (shower, toilet and washbasin).

The flat was ideal for us, and we signed up there and then, paying a 'bond' amounting to a month's rent (insurance against damage, and refunded at the end of tenancy if none), plus a month's rent in advance. This made quite a dent in our savings, but we still had to get ourselves a bed so that we could move in as soon as possible. We found a furniture store and bought a double bed and some pillows which were delivered that afternoon. We also telephoned the storage company who were holding our packing cases, and they delivered them that afternoon too. So we had a bed, pillows, some new (but musty) bedding, packing cases to use as tables, and a cooker for meals—what more could we need? We returned to the hotel, paid for our one night's stay and collected our suitcases. Then we caught a tram on *St George's Terrace* to travel the short journey back to *Adelaide Terrace*—to the first 'home of our own' in our new country. We felt ourselves very lucky that things had fallen into place so well and were very optimistic about our future in this warm, sunny and friendly city of *Perth, Western Australia.*

Sandra on grass by the Swan River,
with South Perth in the distance

There was a small shop next to the office, and we bought a few essential supplies. Then—first things first—we had to Christen our new dwelling, so found an old saucepan to make a cup of tea. We lit the gas, and almost immediately the biggest cockroach we had ever seen crawled our from the back of the cooker! I screamed and ran out of the flat, and wouldn't return until Geoff had killed it. I made him search the rest of the flat for any more 'creepy crawlies' before I could relax and drink that welcome cup of tea.

It wasn't our only encounter with giant native insects whilst living in the flat. One day we saw a two-inch-long hornet hovering outside our bedroom window. Geoff opened the window cautiously, and saw a hornet's nest attached to the wall just below the windowsill. He found a big stick, opened the window slightly, knocked it off the wall and slammed the window shut! This crude method of pest control seemed to work well, and we saw no more hornets. Cockroaches and spiders were another matter entirely . . . .

Before we could shop for food we needed to purchase a refrigerator. It was now mid-summer in Perth, and the temperature was over 100°F (38°C) every day. Any Australians we met always asked "Is it hot enough for you?" or said, "This isn't hot—it was 106° last week." After six weeks of the sunshine and unrelenting heat, we were praying for some cool, refreshing rain.

There was a noticeboard in the covered courtyard of the flats, with notes of items for sale, and we found a medium-sized second-hand 'fridge for $60. It was well worth the money, and we sold it for the same price twelve months later! We could now stock up with essentials and set out to find the nearest supermarket and butcher's shop. We had no car yet, so walked across *The Causeway*, a road crossing the *Swan River*, connecting the city with the eastern suburb of *Victoria Park*. It was only a distance of about one kilometre, but we had set off in the hottest part of the day, and before long a car stopped to offer us a lift—we obviously stood out as newcomers because, as the saying goes, only "Mad Dogs and Englishmen" go out in the mid-day sun! We declined the offer with thanks, but found our way to the nearest watering-hole for a much-needed cold drink. We had a lot to learn about living and working in a hot climate.

At that time the cost of living in Australia was much lower than back in Britain, especially relating to food. Although we had left Britain in the sixties and standards of housing and food supplies were much improved since the early post-war years, we were amazed by the variety of foods available here, especially the meat—whole windows full of every type and cut you could imagine, and although dairy foods, such as milk, cream and cheese tasted quite different, we soon became used to them. Our closest supermarket was in *Hay Street*, which runs parallel to *Adelaide Terrace*, called 'Tom the Cheap'—and it certainly was—we could buy a week's supply of groceries for $8—unbelievable now.

Our block of flats was next to a pub, *The Ozone Hotel*, and we could see into the lounge from our kitchen window. This was handy when we arranged to meet our friends Barbara and Roy there, and could see when they had arrived. One outdated custom still very much alive in Australia in the sixties was that of women not being allowed in the bars of pubs and hotels—they had to drink in the 'Ladies Lounge', although men could drink in there too. Although the females in our group were opposed to this ridiculous rule in principle, it didn't really affect us, as we enjoyed the novelty of sitting outside in the warm evenings for most of the year, with the men sharing jugs of beer and the women drinking lager or wine. My favourite tipple at the time was a 'port and lemon' (port and lemonade), but when asking for this in Australian pubs, I was given a measure of port with a slice of lemon floating on top—the height of Aussie sophistication at the time!

Now that we had a roof over our heads it was time to look for work. This was to prove much harder than we had anticipated, given the time of year and the type of work available, but we were optimistic that it wouldn't take us too long to earn a living in this country full of opportunities.

9

Looking for work (Perth)

It was now January 1968, and most Australians were on a three-week summer break, including Christmas and New Year holidays. Perth's shops, offices and banks were back in business as usual though by early January. Geoff and I were willing to take any work available, and scoured the newspapers for anything suitable. I was looking for clerical work initially, but there was nothing available at that time and with Geoff having worked in industry, we could see things were going to be difficult.

We had kept in touch with our friends from the ship, Barbara and Roy and Anne and Tommy, all of whom had been placed in the now infamous migrant hostels outside the city. These were camps set up to house hundreds of immigrant families. Some were put into wooden shacks and others into ex-army Nissen huts, divided in half, and all with outside communal washing and toilet facilities. These conditions were a harsh introduction to life in Australia, and those who could left as soon as possible. Our friends found flats to rent quickly, and Roy was soon employed as a painter and decorator. Employment wasn't proving so easy to find for the rest of us however, but Anne and a friend had found some part-time work that they thought might interest me too. It was waitressing at *The Grand Hotel* on *St George's Terrace*, and I jumped at the chance to earn some money, as our savings by now were practically non-existent. I went along with the two girls, was interviewed and accepted. I was given a frilly white apron and lace cap, and told that I had to provide my own black dress. On reporting for duty the next day I was told that my 'little black dress' was too short! (It was the sixties). The work was fun—we mostly served at parties and weddings in the afternoons and evenings—though I did feel a bit silly when the lights were put out as we carried flaming 'Baked Alaskas' above our heads into the party venue to the cheers of the guests. However, as welcome as this employment was, Geoff and I both needed full-time jobs to secure our future.

Geoff found his first job soon afterwards. Anne's husband, Tommy, was working at *Forward Down Engineering*, a company based in *Welshpool* a few miles south-east of *Perth*. Geoff caught a bus there, and he was set on as a boiler-maker's assistant, to start the next day. He had never done heavy physical work like this before, labouring in temperatures over 100°F every day. The company produced oil tanks for the oil refineries in *Kwinana,* 28 miles south of *Perth.* Geoff's job was to help the boiler-maker assemble the tanks, hammering the seams straight ready for welding. When the huge metal sheets were separated prior to assembling, all manner of insects ran for cover—and it was Geoff's first sighting of many tiny but deadly red-back spiders which lurked between them. His Italian workmate carried a little wooden hammer in his belt specifically for killing them! There were many nationalities working there—a few Australians, but also Italians, Dutch, Greek and British. The work was done inside open-ended hangers. It was hard work in the intense heat, and by the time Geoff came home he was dirty, hot and exhausted, but with muscles bursting out of his shirt!

My own next foray into the world of employment proved to be a strange and disturbing experience. I applied for a position as receptionist/clerical assistant for a travel agency in the city centre. The interview went well, and it was arranged that I start the next week. The company was owned by a Greek family, with two brothers running the business with the help of another young female assistant. It was a quiet start to the week, giving time for me to be shown around the office, the booking systems and payment methods. At lunch-time the senior partner explained that they usually bought in food from the nearby shops and ate together, so we feasted on fresh rolls, cheese and fruit, followed by coffee. It was a very friendly atmosphere, and I thought this would be an enjoyable full-time position for the foreseeable future. After lunch business was still slow, with nothing for me to do. For some reason the owner/manager showed me the wages book, revealing details of the previous employee's take-home pay. He showed me how much she had earned in overtime, and it did seem that good money could be earned—it would certainly help us to start our savings afresh.

The next day customers were still sparse—most people calling in were friends and business associates of the owners. The staff were as friendly to me as ever, but the time dragged with nothing to do. It might have been the time of year when people were not making travel plans, but I couldn't see that there would be enough work for the four of us, even in busy periods. On the third day, and after being shown the wages book a second time, with emphasis on the 'overtime' earnings, I became very uneasy. The next morning I rang in to say that I wouldn't be returning, and didn't expect any pay for the three days—after all, I had done no work! I was relieved to have made the decision, but I was out of work again, so it was back to the drawing board!

In the meantime, although Geoff was enjoying his stint as a manual labourer, he found the travelling and heat on top of the physical work exhausting, and looked for something closer to home. He soon found a job at *Western Knitters* in east *Perth*. The company produced circular fabric for t-shirts and sweatshirts. It was a small firm and the work was more in Geoff's area of expertise. However the machines were very old, and he really disliked working shifts of 6am— 2pm and 2pm—10 pm. Most of the employees were Australians, with two Aboriginal girls in the making-up department and an Aboriginal handyman, who opened up the factory and undertook general maintenance. There was also a mechanic, Vic, from *Nottingham* in the *Midlands*, who Geoff kept in touch with when he left after two months to work at *Ingrams Batteries* in *Victoria Park*. Geoff's position here was in the workshop, where they assembled batteries for motor vehicles. He also drove a van to deliver the batteries to garages in the vicinity. It was a small, friendly retail area, with a hairdressing shop next door, a school opposite where Rolf Harris had worked in the past as an art teacher, and next to that 'The Pie Shop', which sold meat and fruit pies, bread and pastries. One day Geoff and his workmates heard sirens and saw police cars and an ambulance outside this shop, and heard later that a young girl had had a terrible accident, catching her hand and arm in the mixing machine, and losing her arm up to the elbow. One of those dreadful things you never forget . . . .

During this time I found myself a more stable full-time position working for the *Chamber of Mines* on *St George's Terrace.* There were two managers who would come and go during the day, but mostly I was left to run the office on my own. It wasn't too busy, but I had enough to do to keep me occupied. It was lonely though, and not a good way to make friends. The office was situated on the ground floor of a huge block towards the rear of the building. There was another office close by, and I occasionally chatted to the receptionist there. She was Australian and gave me occasional help and advice. One of the things she told me was, "If your boss asks you if you have any Durex, don't take offence—he means sticky tape (Sellotape)"! Another lesson learned, this time about the peculiarities of a shared, but slightly different, language!

The offices and shops were all air-conditioned—rather too much really, as there was a need for extra layers of clothing inside, and then it was a huge shock to emerge into the heat on the streets. I took my lunch-break at mid-day and became quite familiar with the wide shopping malls, with big stores like *Myers* and *David Jones*.

There was also a quaint English-style shopping arcade leading from *St George's Terrace* through to *Hay Street* called 'London Court'. It has small specialist shops selling souvenirs, crafts, clothing and jewellery—the latter featuring beautiful Australian opals and diamonds—SO tempting! On only our second day in *Perth*, we bought Geoff some shorts from a shop there, and on hearing our accents the assistant asked where we were from. When we replied "Leicester" she was amazed and exclaimed, "I'm from Leicester too—I've been here for 15 years, and you are the first people I've met from my home town!"

There were many lovely small cafés for lunch too—I often called into one for my favourite cheese and tomato toasted sandwich. At first I felt uncomfortable eating on my own, but became used to it, and would take a book or magazine to read. It made for a long, lonely day though, and I still hoped to find some more stimulating work, preferably in larger premises with colleagues for company. Geoff and I were thinking that maybe *Perth* was not the best place for us after all, and we had a decision to make about our future.

10

Earthquake!

Now that we had both secured permanent employment, we were able to make our living accommodation more comfortable. We bought a small table and two chairs for the kitchen, and two sofas for the sitting room, in a dark green velour fabric—not very aesthetically pleasing, but comfortable. We were near enough to walk into the city centre if we were feeling energetic, or we could catch a tram. The trams had large hooks at the back which puzzled us, until we saw a young mum at the tram stop take her baby out of its pram, hook the pram onto the back of the tram, then climb aboard with her baby! Very convenient, as long as everything loose was also removed. If we walked along *Adelaide Terrace* into the city, we always stopped to admire the Spitfire plane mounted outside the RAAF (Royal Australian Air Force) recruiting office. Geoff was told that it was one of the last made with five-blade propellors.

We loved to get letters from 'home' to catch up with the news from family and friends, but with letters taking a week to ten days each way, the news was a bit old by the time we received it. My mum wrote often, and my sister Pat also kept in touch. After we'd been in Perth about three months, she sent a beautiful studio photo of our nephew, Tony and niece, Sharan. It made me cry to think we were missing seeing them grow up. Our sister-in-law Ann also wrote regularly, and we especially enjoyed reading about the exploits of 'little' Geoff! We didn't have a telephone to keep in touch, but neither did any of the family, so letters became very important.

One piece of correspondence we received was quite a shock. It came in a brown envelope just a few weeks after we had arrived in *Perth*, and was from the Australian Government, addressed to Geoff and containing call-up papers for the Australian army! Australian forces at that time were being deployed to *Vietnam*, and this was definitely something we didn't expect to be involved in when considering a new life 'down under'! Australian soldiers were being recruited by ballot, and Geoff's name had been drawn out. (If only he was that lucky with the Lottery). I wrote a letter on Geoff's behalf explaining our circumstances—that we had somewhere to live, but no permanent employment as yet—therefore it would leave me alone and unemployed (with no benefits), and we had a reply agreeing to defer call-up—thankfully we never heard from them again!

One Sunday morning in October while relaxing in the flat, we heard a strange rumbling sound and everything began to shake. Pictures were falling from the walls and ornaments from the shelves. We ran outside to see what was causing this disturbance, along with many other residents, and were warned to get clear of the buildings as it was an earthquake! I foolishly ran back to shut our front door!

When we returned to our flat about half-an-hour later we found cracks in the plaster on the walls, and some broken picture frames and ornaments. I was particularly upset that a long-necked black cat was broken in half, as this was a gift and a reminder of 'home'. This was a new and frightening experience for most residents of the flats, but the Australians, in their typical laid-back manner, dismissed it as "just a tremor" which, they said, happened quite often as a result of mining operations outside the city. We found out later that the epicentre of the earthquake (measuring 6.9 on the *Richter Scale*—hardly a 'tremor'), was in *Meckering*, about 75 miles east of *Perth*—a small town of just 240 residents at that time. Most of the brick-built dwellings were flattened, but amazingly the wooden houses remained virtually intact. The railway lines into the town were buckled, and there were huge wide, deep fissures in the roads and countryside. Miraculously, although there had been some injuries, there was no loss of life. It was all over so quickly that we didn't realise how significant and damaging this earthquake had been. It is still recorded as one of the largest in Australia's history.

The next day when most of the population of *Perth* was back at work, there were some 'aftershocks' felt in the city. I was in my office alone, and the walls were shaking around me. This was much more frightening than the original earthquake because I knew what it was this time, but it seemed to be expected as a 'settling down' of the land after such an upheaval. I wished I could be with Geoff, and was so relieved when it was time to go home. I'm pleased to say that we never experienced anything like this again during the rest of our time in Australia.

There was a police station close by, between *Adelaide Terrace* and *Hay Street*, and we had reason to summon them to the flat concerning a matter of theft—not from our flat itself, but from our washing line in the courtyard—several items of my underwear had been stolen! Two officers came, guns on hips, to 'take down my particulars'! One was quite young, and when I blushingly gave them details of the items stolen— one being a girdle (made of firm elastic to keep the stomach in, and stockings up)—the young man said, "What's a girdle?" His middle-aged colleague gave him a withering look and said, "I'll explain later." We never heard from them again, and my missing lingerie was never found.

It was nearing Christmas-time again, and the temperature was climbing up to around 90°F every day, with cloudless, sunny skies. It was strange to be so warm at this time of year, and to be buying presents for friends and family back in cold, dark and frosty Britain. We bought the usual Aussie souvenirs—furry koalas and kangaroos, wooden carved boomerangs, purses (made from kangaroo hide and fur), and inexpensive jewellery containing Australian opal chips.

On Christmas Eve 1968 a *Salvation Army* band arrived in the courtyard of the flats to play hymns and carols—a wonderful surprise, and much appreciated by everyone. They were standing on the back of a flat trailer, and were a colourful sight in their navy and red uniforms, and with their shiny brass instruments—a real Christmas treat.

Meanwhile, we hadn't forgotten Mr Calwell's advice about investing in land, and we purchased a block of land as part of a syndicate in *Rockingham*, a costal town 40km (28 miles) south-west of *Perth*. The plot was an acre and cost us $750, which we paid for by monthly instalments. This made us feel we were making a real commitment to our new country—the first step to putting down roots.

11

Fun and games

It wasn't all work and no play during our time in Perth. There were the usual recreational things to do in the city—we saw 'Guess Who's Coming to Dinner?' (Sidney Poitier!) at the cinema, and also 'Fiddler on the Roof' at the theatre, starring Topal, but sadly we could only afford tickets up in the 'gods'! We were now ready to explore further afield and so Geoff booked some driving lessons with an instructor, Helen, who was using the proceeds of these hourly sessions to take flying lessons. After a few weeks, Geoff was ready to take his test. It was a very informal process in those days—undertaken by the police force. Geoff duly arrived at the station, and a big, burly sergeant, with his newspaper under his arm, climbed into the front passenger seat. He settled down to read the paper, and told Geoff to set off. With a few instructions to turn left and right, they returned to the station, where Geoff completed a parallel parking manoeuvre, and the officer said: "You'll do"—and wrote out his pass certificate. We then searched for our first car—and settled on an old green *Simca 1.3* for $400.

We could now go to see a 'drive-in' movie, which was something we had been really keen to do. It was quite a different experience from an indoor cinema—you paid the entrance fee, drove up to a parking space, wound down the driver's window, took a large speaker from a post and attached it to the car door. The advantages of the 'drive-in' were that you could either buy food and drink from kiosks there, or take your own (and no complaints about rustling sweet wrappers!). Also couples with young children could dress them in their nightwear and bundle them into the back seat of the car to sleep—no need for babysitters! The first film we saw at a drive-in cinema was 'Grand Prix' starring James Garner—I had to remind Geoff that he wasn't on a race track on the drive home!

When we were feeling particularly homesick we would drive out to *Perth Airport* on Sunday mornings to get the English newspapers, and to watch the planes come and go. We would soon snap out of it though, and find new places to visit. We knew we had to persevere and try our hardest to settle down—especially as if we didn't stay in Australia for two years, we would have to pay back the cost of our fares. I think this was a good ploy by the Immigration Service, as it does take a long time to feel 'at home', however lovely the place and friendly the natives may be.

Our nearest beach was called 'City Beach', which was also the name of the suburb. It has soft white sand and sand dunes, and is a lovely place to relax and watch the swimmers and surfers in the sparkling blue *Indian Ocean*. One Sunday morning we were listening to the local radio station when it was announced that there was a huge shoal of sea salmon swimming just off the beach. We jumped into our car and arrived in time to see a dozen or so fishermen standing at the edge of the sea, casting into the surf and pulling out thrashing, silvery salmon one after the other. These were thrown into the open backs of pick-up trucks, which were soon overflowing. We were told they would be sold for pet food. It was an amazing sight on that hot, sunny morning.

On another Sunday morning at the same beach, Geoff was swimming with friends, and I was sunbathing close to some sand dunes. I heard a rustling sound behind me and just a few inches away sitting on a rock, was a frill-necked lizard (dragon). He was about 18-20" long, with a dark brownish body (for camouflage), but the brightest orangey-red frill all around his head, which these lizards inflate when they feel threatened. We looked at each other for a few seconds, and then he scurried away. Another wonderful new experience for me, and a close encounter I wouldn't forget.

There are many pretty parks and gardens in *Perth*, our nearest being *Queens Gardens* on *Hay Street*, a lovely oasis in the middle of the busy city. There are green lawns, several lakes—some stocked with a variety of fish, bridges connecting walkways, and colourful flowerbeds showcasing Australian native flora, including golden *wattle*, the distinctive red and green *Kangaroo's Paw*, and also a variety of delicate orchids. In the centre of the park is a replica statue of *Peter Pan* by the sculptor of the original statue in *Kensington Gardens*, *London* (Sir George Frampton), and signed by the creator of *Peter Pan*, Sir J M Barrie. The lawns were kept lovely and green in the hot, dry climate of Western Australia with constant watering, but the grass was very coarse 'buffalo' grass—hard to walk on in bare feet—very different from the soft 'green, green grass of home'.

Perth Zoo is located in *South Perth*, and is a wonderful place to visit to see native and exotic animals spread over 17 hectares (41 acres). Besides the well-known symbols of Australia, such as *kangaroos*, *koalas* and *emus*, the strangest creature we saw was a '*duck-billed platypus*', which, when a specimen was first taken back to England in the 18th century, was thought to be a trick combination of several creatures. It is a mammal, 30-45cm (11-17") long, with a black bill like a duck, a long, brown furry body, a flat tail like a beaver, and webbed feet. It has a spur on its hind legs which can inject venom—very painful to humans, and sometimes fatal to other creatures. They live on land, but swim to catch their food. It is the only mammal which lays eggs. A very cute and fascinating creature.

Behind our block of flats was a green open space leading down to the *Swan River*, and we could see over the water to *South Perth*. The *Swan Brewery* was built on the banks of the *Swan River* (both named after the native *black swans* of Australia—another fascinating Australian species). The building was lit up at night by hundreds of lights outlining the shape of a ship, seemingly floating on the water. This brewery produced the local *Swan* and *Emu* beers, but sadly has now been replaced by a restaurant and apartments, and the relocated brewery is closing, with production moving to *South Australia*.

We had a wonderful day out with friends at *Yanchep National Park*, 42km (26 miles) north of *Perth*. It is an area of natural bushland covering 2,842 hectares (7,022 acres), with walking trails, ancient *caves*, *koala* colonies, *kangaroos*, *wallabies* and hundreds of nesting *cockatoos*. There are picnic areas with wooden tables and benches, and free gas barbecues. We took our own meat and salad in an *Esky* (cool box)— an essential piece of equipment to take on any car journey—a true-blue Aussie wouldn't go anywhere without one—or preferably two—one for food and one for beer! There's nothing quite like a barbecue of steak and sausages under the warm sun, surrounded by the distinctive-smelling eucalyptus trees and with the wildlife and colourful birds all around—though the flies and mosquitos could be a real nuisance.

Geoff had a great time with Roy, Tommy and Roger (who worked with Roy) on a trip to *Mandurah Weir*, 72 km (45 miles) south of *Perth*. They hired a boat to fish for crabs, and used a sheep's head for bait! It was a successful day— they filled a paint drum with '*blue manna' crabs*, the largest being at least two feet across. One escaped the drum, and caused havoc, snapping at their bare toes. They cooked some in a drum of boiling water for their lunch. Later in the day while they were anchored out at sea, they looked across to a sandbank and saw a blanket of pink in the distance. On closer investigation they discovered it was a flock of hundreds of *flamingos* feeding in the shallows, their long legs and vibrant deep pink plumage creating a memorable image in the late afternoon sun.

We enjoyed regular parties and barbecues with friends, and even attended a dinner dance at 'The Italian Club', which put on a special 'Blackpool Ball' for homesick ex-pats. Our circle of friends was expanding too—in particular we met 'Prof', Jim and 'Knocker', three young single men who had come out to Australia in 1965 on the *Castel Felice*. They were desperate to meet young single women, but at that time females were in a minority in Australia, and as a result, any young, marriageable female found herself very popular!

Despite making some wonderful friends, and seeing many wonderful sights in *Perth* and further afield in the huge state of *Western Australia*, (not to mention the great weather—too hot at times, but we hadn't once needed to wear a coat—and only occasionally needed an umbrella!) Geoff and I had not found our ideal jobs, and so, after almost a year living in Perth, we began to make plans to explore pastures new.

12

Melbourne here we come!

Geoff and his friend Vic had kept in touch since Geoff had left *Western Knitters*. Vic and his wife Margaret had lived in Perth since arriving from the UK in 1965, and had a lovely house—a 3-bedroom bungalow, typical of suburban homes in Australia. They had a baby daughter and two white poodles, and seemed to have a comfortable life, but Vic, like Geoff, was unsettled at work. He and Geoff obtained newspapers from *Sydney*, the capital of *New South Wales* on the east coast, and *Melbourne*, the capital of *Victoria* on the south east coast, and scoured them looking for job opportunities. The *Melbourne Herald* had a 30-page supplement of vacancies, with literally hundreds of situations available in the textile industry. There were also many clerical positions advertised, and so when Geoff asked me if I would be happy to move to *Melbourne*, I agreed immediately. Vic had also persuaded his wife that relocating to *Melbourne* would be the best for them too, so together we made plans to travel to the other side of Australia. Vic wanted to drive to Melbourne in his blue *Mark II Cortina*—a distance of 3420km (2125 miles—the equivalent of driving from London, England to Moscow in Russia), while his wife planned to fly over (3 hr 20 min) with their baby and dogs once he had found temporary accommodation for them all. Geoff and I were keen to see some of 'outback' Australia, and we arranged to travel with Vic, with Geoff sharing the driving. So a new adventure awaited us, and all we had to do was give our notice at work, sell our few belongings—including the car, (which a friend Ted bought for $100), and we were once again homeless and jobless (but not quite penniless), travelling into the unknown.

On 28th December 1968—exactly a year since arriving in Perth—we set off on our epic trip. The car roof rack was loaded with an extra spare wheel, a can of petrol and water containers, with suitcases, sleeping bags and food crammed into every spare space inside the car. It was advised that travellers undertaking this possibly perilous journey should report to the police authorities before setting out, giving details of the intended route (there was only one road!), and estimated time of arrival at their destination. We foolishly ignored this advice—after all, what could possibly go wrong on this 2,000-mile journey across the south of Australia, most of which would be across desert, on unmade roads, with 'road houses' for refreshment and petrol every 200-300 miles apart?!

We left the city of *Perth* and travelled east through small, remote country towns, looking exactly like those seen in American cowboy movies—wooden 2-storey buildings with verandahs overlooking the main street, to join the *Eyre Highway*, which we would be travelling on for 1,041 miles of our journey—the link between *Perth* and *Port Augusta*, north of *Adelaide*, the capital of *South Australia*. This highway was constructed in 1941 and named after *Edward John Eyre*, an English explorer who led expeditions to find suitable sheep and cattle grazing land—the first European, with his Aboriginal friend Wylie and others, to cross southern Australia on foot from east to west via the *Nullarbor Plain* a hundred years before.

Once we joined the *Eyre Highway* at *Norseman,* south of *Kalgoorlie*, we felt that our journey had really begun. This 'highway' covered 2695km (1675 miles)—about two-thirds of the distance to our final destination—the city of *Melbourne*. At that time it was a wide, mostly unmade road, with frequent potholes seeming to appear out of nowhere, some big enough to swallow a car! It is situated along the south coast of Australia, following the *Great Australian*

Bight to the south, with the *Nullarbor Plain* to the north—200,000 square kilometres of limestone, covered in sparse vegetation, and beyond that the remote *Great Victoria Desert*.

Our journey across the *Nullarbor* (Latin for 'no trees') was quite an experience. The road ahead was long and straight and disappeared into a heat haze, and on either side all we could see to the horizon was sandy, reddish, saltbush-covered terrain. The men took turns driving—keeping up to a speed of 50mph, which was the fastest we could travel on the rough surface, for hour after hour straight ahead, leaving a cloud of red dust in our wake. Whoever was not driving would stretch out on the back seat to rest and catch up with some sleep, while I sat in the front passenger seat chatting to the driver to keep him awake and alert during the monotonous hours. Every few hundred miles we came across a 'roadhouse'—a petrol station on the edge of the highway, and if we were lucky, a pub! We were very glad of these 'comfort breaks' to use the facilities, fill up with petrol and purchase some food and to have a brief chat, but with the temperature outside the car being over 100°F, the engine would heat up rapidly, and we had to quickly set off again! We rarely saw other cars travelling either way. From *Caiguna Roadhouse* to *Balladonia Roadhouse* there is the longest stretch of straight road in Australia, called the '90-mile straight'.

A brief stop on the Eyre Highway

We covered nearly 400 miles on our first day, and were all tired and hungry by nightfall. We were in the middle of the wilderness, and the temperature had dropped dramatically, but the sky was clear, and the moonlight illuminated the surrounding bush. We had pulled just off the highway and we carefully built a fire with stones surrounding it, and made ourselves some tea in a billy can. We felt like real explorers—but drew the line at actually sleeping on the ground after Geoff spotted a 'trapdoor' spider nearby—who knew what else was lurking in the undergrowth? We were all travelling with our trousers tucked into our socks to prevent anything crawling upwards!

We spent the night in the car, which was a bit of a squeeze, with the men taking turns sleeping stretched out across the back seat, while I curled up in the front passenger seat.

We set off bright and early the next morning while it was still fairly cool, and continued our long, seemingly endless, journey across the *Nullarbor.* We still hadn't seen many humans on our trip, or wildlife for that matter, but one episode really brightened our day. Geoff was driving along the centre of the highway, mainly to avoid the potholes, and from out of the bush on his right ran one, two, then three emus! Geoff slowed down as they were joined by three more long-legged feathered friends. They ran alongside the car for about two hundred yards, and then veered back into the scrub. Emus are related to ostriches, but smaller at around five feet tall, mostly brown in colour, with big, beady eyes—scary but comical at the same time!

We were fast approaching the *Western Australia/South Australia* border. Ahead of us in the distance we could see what looked like hills of snow—on closer inspection these turned out to be fine, white sand dunes, with the remains of a historic telegraph station sticking up above the mounds, and a sign informing us that this was *Eucla,* and that the border was just eight miles away. There was nothing else to see at that time, but today *Eucla* is a tourist attraction on this famous road trip across the *Nullarbor*, with a hotel, restaurant, golf club and museum. We soon reached the border, and took each others photos at the signpost planted in the earth at the edge of the road, with still no sightings of civilisation. We had to travel approximately 1,600 km (994 miles) to reach the *South Australian/Victorian* border, and we kept up our speed to cover as many miles as possible before nightfall. We managed to cover over 700 miles on our second day, and once again prepared for a second night sleeping in the car, just outside the town of *Ceduna.* Although it was mid-summer, it was cold overnight, and after a cup of billy tea and some sandwiches, we bedded down for the night. One thing that took some getting used to in Australia was the lack of 'dusk'—that time between day and night, which in the northern hemisphere during the summer months can last for an hour, but in the southern half of the world, light to dark is almost immediate.

At sunrise the next morning we drove the short distance to the small town of *Ceduna*, where we tucked into a hearty breakfast in a very welcome roadhouse. When we returned to the car, there were dozens of small birds, mostly sparrows, pecking at the insects embedded in the front grill. We hadn't realised until this point how we had missed seeing the humble sparrow, as in *Western*

Australia they had been deliberately culled because they were considered a threat to crops, and they are still considered a pest today. As well as our usual supplies, we were able to purchase newspapers at this latest 'watering hole', and were eager to catch up on any happenings around the world while we had been in the wilderness. One piece of news that we were really happy to know was that *Sophia Loren* had at last given birth to a baby boy the day before—*Carlo Ponti Jnr*, after many years of trying. We were very pleased for her, though it does seem strange that this was the only piece of world news that we remember from that time.

We were now on the last leg of our journey on the *Eyre Highway*, and it was a great relief to Geoff and Vic that this last section from *Ceduna* to *Port Augusta* where the highway ended, was tarmac-ed. It made for much faster travelling, though the scenery changed little, and rather than mainly following the coastline, the highway cut directly west to east across the north of the *Eyre Peninsula*. *Port Augusta* is 300km (186 miles) north of *Adelaide*, and is a thriving commercial centre and port. It also has a *Royal Flying Doctor Service*, one of 14 centres around Australia supplying healthcare to people living in the Australian *Outback*. After leaving *Port Augusta* we travelled south towards *Adelaide*. The roads were much smoother now, and we made good time. We drove around the outskirts of the city as it was getting dark, and had wonderful views overlooking the lights of *Adelaide* from the surrounding hills. We carried on travelling for another two or three hundred miles as the roads were so much better, and decided to spend our third—and hopefully last—night sleeping in the car just off the beaten track.

The next morning—31st December 1968, we eagerly headed east on the *Princes Highway*, with the end of our mammoth journey in sight. We crossed the *South Australia/ Victoria* border, with just the obligatory single signpost, telling us we had approximately 300 miles to go! The roads now were becoming busier, and the trusty *Cortina,* which was just six months old when we set off from *Perth*, made good time, the only trouble being with the electrical system. We entered the outskirts of *Melbourne* in the late afternoon and drove along *St Kilda Road* into the city. There were lush green gardens on the right, and the impressive war memorial (*Shrine of Remembrance*) at a junction, which can be seen travelling either into or out of the city. The temperature was around 80°F—more comfortable for us, the sun was shining, and there was a lively buzz in this very Metropolitan capital city. We drove into the city centre via *Princes Bridge* over the *Yarra River*, and even at this early stage, we were sure this had been the right move—we were very optimistic about the future.

We found rooms in a cheap motel in the central district (I was given a very funny look by the proprietor when I arrived looking very dishevelled, with two unkempt men!), and then we went out to get our bearings in this vibrant city. It was New Year's Eve, and people were gathering to celebrate in the many parks and gardens. At the stroke of midnight all the cars tooted their horns, and fireworks exploded all around us. What a wonderful welcome!

13

Employment in Melbourne

Melbourne is often called 'The Garden City', which we certainly saw evidence of during our first forays around the centre and suburbs. Founded in 1835, it was declared a city by Queen Victoria in 1847—becoming the capital of the Colony (now State) of *Victoria* in 1851. The population was swelled by migrants from Ireland, Germany and China (the Chinese founding their own 'Chinatown' in 1851), and the *Gold Rush* of that same year increased the population from 25,000 to 40,000 in just a few months. Post-war immigration from Britain and Europe further increased the population, and when we arrived there at the end of 1968 this was nearly three million. Today there are over four million residents in greater *Melbourne*, which covers an area of over 2,000 square kilometres.

Melbourne has excellent transport systems in and out of the city—including buses, the world's largest tram network, and train services, connecting streets and suburbs—all complementing each other and making it relatively easy to move around this large city. The facade of the main entrance to *Flinders Street Station,* with its dome, arched entrance and clocks is one of the most recognisable landmarks of *Melbourne.* In 2011/12 *Melbourne* was voted 'the world's most liveable city', and we certainly found it to be just that in our years working and bringing up a family there.

It was 1st January 1969—a national holiday— and families were out in force enjoying picnics and music in the city parks and the beautiful *Botanical Gardens,* which lead down to the *River Yarra*, where colourful canoes and pleasure boats sailed up and down, brightening up this strangely brown-coloured river. On the city centre side of the river there was an open-air art exhibition, with paintings by local artists at very reasonable prices, situated on the boundary of *Fitzroy Gardens*—64 acres of landscaped gardens on the southeastern edge of *Melbourne's Central Business District* (CBD), containing a lake, café, model Tudor village, fountains and the 'Fairies Tree'—a tree trunk of a Red Gum over 300 years old—carved by *Ola Cohn* into a delightful tribute to Australia's native creatures, including koalas and flying foxes, but with the addition of fairies, dwarves and gnomes, which give it a special place in the hearts of the visiting children. These gardens are also the 'new' location of *Captain Cook's cottage*, which was originally built in

Yorkshire, England in 1755, and for a short time was the childhood home of *Captain James Cook*. Because of *Captain Cook*'s connection with Australia, the cottage was purchased in 1933 by *Russell Grimwald,* who donated the house to the people of *Victoria*. It was dismantled and rebuilt in *Fitzroy Gardens* in 1934 to celebrate the state of *Victoria*'s centenary.

After another night spent in our very basic accommodation, we set out to find ourselves something more permanent. We wanted to be close to the city and transport, as all three of us would be seeking work, and we were lucky to find a two-bedroom flat on the corner of *Dandenong Road* and *Orrong Road*, in the suburb of *East St Kilda*. *Dandenong Road* is a very wide thoroughfare, leading on to *St Kilda Road* towards the city one way, and eastwards out to the *Dandenong Ranges*. It has three lanes either side for regular traffic, and two-way tram tracks in the centre, bordered each side by trees. It is a very convenient way to get about this big city and its sprawling suburbs.

The flat was at the back of a brick bungalow, with the entrance on *Orrong Road*, and parking space for one car and a small garden at the back. It had a sitting room, one medium and one small bedroom, a small kitchen, and an even smaller bathroom. We could see it would be quite cramped for all of us, but Vic telephoned his wife immediately, and his family were soon on their way to join him. On arrival, Margaret agreed it was too small for us all, but it gave them a temporary base while looking for something more suitable. They did find a bigger place to rent for a while, but as they had sold a house in *Perth*, they were able to purchase another in a *Melbourne* suburb, and were soon happily settled. However the flat was perfect for just Geoff and me, with transport on our doorstep, and shops close by on *Orrong Road,* including a milk bar (newsagent), a chemist, bottle shop (off licence) and a laundrette.

Once again we had to search for employment. This proved much easier in the east—jobs were plentiful in the textile industry, as they were in England in the late sixties—it had been possible to walk out of one position in the morning, and have another by the afternoon (as I once proved myself after a disagreement with management), and we hoped it would be the same here. Geoff bought a copy of the *Herald* newspaper and found plenty of positions that would suit him. He saw a vacancy for a flat-frame knitter at a firm called *The Wheel of Fashion*, and caught a tram to the small factory for a brief interview. The company made mostly sweaters, and Geoff was offered the job there and then, to start the next day. The other employees were a mixture of nationalities, including a Brazilian, a Scotsman, and again, someone from Nottingham! Geoff enjoyed working there, although he didn't like having to work three shifts—but it was good to find employment so soon, and to know that we would be able to pay the rent.

In the meantime I was also searching for work. I caught a green-painted tram—just a few steps away on *Dandenong Road*, and travelled into central *Melbourne*—about 30 minutes traveling time. I had a list of job agencies in the city, and called into one on the ground floor of a tall building on *Bourke Street*. They said they had nothing to suit me at that time, but the very helpful staff there thought there might be something available with a firm in the same building—*Elder Smith, Goldsbrough Mort*. I took the lift (which I was to become trapped in on my own for a few hours some months later) to the 23rd floor, and the receptionist took my details. She went off to see the manager, who returned within a few minutes, and after a brief chat he said they did have a clerical position available and was I interested? I certainly was! I was given some details of the position, and agreed to start the next week. I was thrilled to get a job at my first attempt, and couldn't wait to get home to tell Geoff.

Elder Smith Goldsbrough Mort was a large company—general merchants dealing in wool amongst other things. I bought some beautiful pure Merino wool 'Onkaparinga' blankets while I worked there. The office I worked in was large, with around seven other typists and clerical staff, and four or five managers. My main task was to type up the letters handwritten by the managers, who would drop them into one box, to be typed up and handed back as soon as possible. At first, not recognising each person's handwriting, I did put the wrong names on a few letters but they were very understanding, and I soon became familiar with each person's style. One particular task I had to undertake was to use a teletype machine to enter figures and information to be distributed country-wide. This was treated as urgent, and would take me about two days each month, sitting in a small office on my own. It was a very unpopular task, but I just got on with it, much to the relief of the other clerks, who found it boring and tiring.

As previously, I found everyone in the office to be friendly and helpful. The Aussies made jokes sometimes about 'Poms', but as long as I didn't take offence, and returned the lighthearted banter, things were fine. Being a fairly new immigrant, I was careful not to complain about little things though—I suppose fearful of being called a 'whinging Pom'. Australians can be very sensitive about certain subjects—sport especially—and in particular *Australian Rules Football.* They are quite fanatical about it, with almost every suburb having their own team, and with as many women supporters as men—some couples even supporting different teams. I made the mistake of repeating something that Geoff had said—"It's not really football, is it?" This went down like a lead balloon—I'm surprised anyone spoke to me after that! The staff were mostly Australian, but there were a couple of English women, and one Welsh, and I was told by the Australians that our accents sounded just the same—I suppose there must be such a thing as a 'British' accent! ESGM had a very active social club, and Geoff and I particularly enjoyed the group nights out to the cinema. One film we particularly enjoyed that year was 'Paint Your Wagon', starring Clint Eastward, Lee Marvin and Jean Seberg. We liked it so much we took my mum to see it over a year later when she came on her first visit to *Melbourne*.

Geoff in the meantime was still looking for his ideal position. The *Herald* again came to the rescue, with a position advertised for a knitting machine operator at *Crestknit* in the suburb of *Hawthorn*, just a short tram ride away. He went for an interview, was offered the job, and started the next Monday. Finding suitable employment was certainly proving easier on this side of Australia. He enjoyed the work but as before, it was shift-work, this time two shifts, an early shift of 6am—3pm, and late shift of 3pm—12pm, working alternate weeks with Stan, a Polish immigrant. Geoff really didn't like working the late shift and was talking of leaving, but the manager had a word with them both, and as Stan preferred the late shift, they agreed to stick to their preferred hours, which worked out very well for them both.

Crestknit was a large textile company, making mostly knitwear and fabric, and it employed many nationalities in the factory—apart from quite a few Australians, there were Polish, Spanish, Greek, Dutch, Chinese and English, including one man, George (from Nottingham!), and Jim (from Leicester—hooray!) Quite a few of his workmates were postwar refugees, who told Geoff some interesting and sometimes harrowing, stories: Stan (Polish): He escaped from *Poland* when the Germans invaded, and joined the *Russian* army, where he was treated quite badly. He made his way to an *Austrian* refugee camp when the war ended. He was then offered a choice of going to *Argentina* or *Australia*, and knowing nothing about either country, he chose Australia—because they spoke English! He spent some time in *Bonegilla Migrant Camp* in north-east *Victoria,* before moving south to *Melbourne.* Sam (Polish

Jew): During the war he and his family were in a concentration camp in *Poland*, and he was the sole survivor. He showed Geoff the tattooed identification numbers on his arm. He had arrived in Australia after the war as a refugee, married a Polish Jew and had a son. Benny (Dutch): He had arrived in Australia from an orphanage in *Holland*, and boarded for a while with a family in *Wodonga* on the Victoria/NSW border. Joey (Chinese): He came from an orphanage in *Hong Kong*, and married an Australian girl. Geoff and a few friends from work attended the ceremony at *Malvern Town Hall*. Felix (Polish): Felix came from a wealthy family. During the harsh years of the war, he and his family survived on the proceeds from his mother's jewellery. His mother died during the war, and afterwards his father and sister returned to *Poland*, while Felix travelled on his own to Australia while still a teenager. He married a Polish woman in Australia and had two children. He became a good friend of Geoff. Heinz (German): He worked as a mechanic at *Crestknit*, and had an uneasy working relationship with his colleagues—particularly the Poles (understandably).

Geoff's Australian workmates—Rex, Tiger, Alan, Lance and two Rons, became good friends, and it was a happy working environment. During the eight years he was employed there he rarely received any negative jibes—the only reference to his 'Englishness' was on Friday afternoons, when his Aussie mates would shout—"C'mon you Pommie Bastard—the pub's open!"

14

Out and about in Melbourne

Just two months after arriving in *Melbourne* I celebrated my 21st birthday (on 1st March, as it wasn't a Leap Year). 'Celebrate' is probably not quite the right word—we had left friends and family behind on the other side of the world, moved away from new friends in *Perth* on the other side of Australia, and hadn't had time to make new ones in *Melbourne*. However, I wanted to mark the occasion, so I bought a large cake— shaped in the numbers 2 and 1, and took half to work to share with my colleagues. Geoff and I did go out in the evening with another couple—I had met the English girl at work, but we didn't know them very well, and the evening wasn't a huge success.

One very memorable occasion that year (1969) occurred in July. Geoff was not well—suffering from acute 'flu-like symptoms— so I rang our doctor to arrange a home visit. I took the day off work to play nurse, and to let the doctor in when he arrived. It was 20th July, 1969—the day of the U.S. *Apollo II* landing on the surface of the moon. We put on our small black and white television, and at approximately 11am Melbourne time, we saw the blurry live pictures of Neil Armstrong walking on the moon, and heard those unforgettable words: "That's one small step for man, one giant leap for mankind".

Geoff took a while to recover from his illness— not helped by the cold, damp flat, which even the doctor remarked upon. Although it was mid-winter in Melbourne, the temperature outside was still around 17°C (60°F), but with no central heating and just a small electric fire, it felt quite chilly inside. We even had mildew on our clothes in the wardrobe! Fortunately Australian winters are short and the summers long, so we were soon enjoying warmer weather again.

We loved living so close to the city, and the convenient transport made it easy to explore Melbourne, the suburbs and our closest beaches. *Melbourne*'s wide streets, with large, busy department stores, offices and restaurants linked by small lanes with specialist boutiques and cafés, make shopping in the city a wonderful experience. Within walking distance or a short tram ride are *Melbourne Zoo*; the *Melbourne Museum* (containing, among many interesting artifacts and exhibitions the stuffed remains of *Phar Lap*, a legendary Australian racehorse, who died in 1932 under suspicious circumstances) and the *Royal Exhibition Building* (Great

Hall)—built in 1879, which is a very impressive sight, and is surrounded by beautiful gardens. Over the year events such as car shows, boat shows and trade and fashion shows are featured there. It is now listed as a *World Heritage* site. Among the many attractions *Melbourne* has to offer, I must not forget to mention *Queen Victoria Market*—operating since 1878. It covers a huge open area, with awnings covering the stalls—half of the space dedicated to fresh produce such as meat, chicken, seafood, fresh fruit and vegetables and delicatessan goods. The rest of the market is given over to clothing, shoes, jewellery, arts and crafts, and is also a great place to find inexpensive souvenirs. In the centre is an open-air eating area, where foods of all kinds can be bought and eaten at small tables, including Chinese, Indian, Greek and Italian delicacies, but also the good old fish and chips!

One place not to be missed on any itinerary is the *Old Melbourne Gaol* on *Russell Street*, where the bushranger *Ned Kelly* was hanged in 1880. He was convicted of murder, and after his death his head was removed and a death mask made, which can be viewed inside the gaol, along with the scaffold, and also some of his armour—a helmet and breastplate—which visitors can try on (and be photographed in!) Several films have been made about the exploits of Ned and his gang, in particular one made in 1970 starring Mick Jagger (of *The Rolling Stones* fame), which, though not a brilliant portrayal of the convict, did bring his story to a wider audience.

Closer to home, we had our first taste of pizza—at *Poppa's Pizza* on *High Street, Prahan*. We stood outside in the street, and watched through the window, as the owner made and tossed the dough base in the air to shape it, then decorated it with cheese, tomatoes, and all kinds of meat and vegetables—we couldn't wait to go inside for a taste!

A ten-minute tram ride would take us to *St Kilda*, a beachside suburb, which had lovely small specialty clothes and cake shops, and closer to the beach was *Luna Park* fun fair, with its iconic laughing face entrance and creaking rollercoaster ride. It was built in 1912, the first of five to be built in different Australian cities. It has been renovated many times over the years, with some rides and attractions taken away and others added, but it retains the old-fashioned 'fun-of-the-fair' atmosphere. It is another of *Melbourne*'s *World Heritage* sites.

St Kilda's *Upper Esplanade* has views over the sandy beaches, and on Sunday mornings a craft fair is held here, with around thirty stalls selling hand-made leather bags, jewellery, ceramics, wooden carvings, and many authentic

Aboriginal artifacts, including boomerangs and didgeridoos—all beautifully decorated. There is always an amazing display of paintings by local artists too. It became one of my favourite sunny Sunday morning outings, and was a wonderful place for buying birthday and Christmas gifts for family and friends back in England. Much as we liked *St Kilda* though, it was not a place to linger after dark, when it became a notorious 'red light' district. Today it is very different, and is now a trendy place, with a vibrant café culture, and is very popular with tourists.

One Saturday morning as we were preparing to go out to do our weekly food shopping, there was a knock at the door. Geoff opened it and was really surprised to see Dave, a friend from *Byfords*, with his wife Anne. Dave was amongst a group of 'bikers' who Geoff used to go out with—Geoff on the back of another friend's bike (Mick) until he bought his own. Later Geoff and I went out regularly with Mick and his girlfriend on their bikes, almost freezing to death in the winter, despite our leather jackets! We had kept in touch with Mick and another of Geoff's workmates, Rodney, and Dave had obtained our address from one of them. Dave and Anne became good friends, and we enjoyed some lovely outings with them—including several visits to the *Harold Holt Memorial Pool* (as mentioned in Chapter 5).

It has a big indoor pool, and outside is a diving pool, a small pool for children, and a large pool surrounded by grass lawns—ideal for picnics. It was wonderful to swim while feeling the warm sun on our backs. It was a standing joke that you could always pick out the newly-arrived migrants, as their skin would be so pale!

Dave had worked as a mechanic in Leicester, and had kept in touch with another ex-Byford employee Tony, who was now working at *Red Robin,* a sock manufacturing firm in *Brunswick*. Dave contacted him on arrival in *Melbourne*, and was soon also employed there. Our circle of friends was growing, and once we bought our next car—a second-hand green (again!) *Morris 1100*, we could explore more of the outskirts of *Melbourne* and the state of *Victoria*. We had a lovely trip out to *The Eltham Barrel Restaurant*—a group of 8—all from Leicester! This huge barrel-shaped restaurant was built on *Main Street, Eltham*, constructed from wood and bricks, with a glass front, and could cater for up to 400 guests. Sadly it is no more—having burnt down over 30 years ago, and replaced by houses. Unfortunately our acquaintance with one of these couples led to hearing one of the most tragic stories imaginable.

Eltham Barrel Restaurant—Leicester friends re-united

Tony and Betty had lived in *Melbourne* a number of years, and had three sons aged 21, 18 and 11. They had bought a block of land in the suburbs, and had a modern house (bungalow) built on it—a popular choice of new home-owners in the sixties and seventies. One evening their two older boys, who had been quarrelling earlier, returned home, and the 19-year-old was in his bedroom when his 21-year-old brother walked in and shot him with a rifle. The bullet pierced the jugular vein in his neck, and he died instantly. It was such a shock to everyone who knew the family, and we couldn't imagine the pain felt by Tony and Betty. The story was in the newspapers, but with no real explanation of what had caused such animosity between the two brothers. The older boy was given a long gaol sentence, and they were left with just their 11-year-old son at home. We did see them a few times afterwards, and of course this tragedy had an enormous effect on them, though Betty did find some comfort in her religion.

Ted, our friend from *Perth*, had married after we left and he and his new wife Olive moved to *Sydney* for a while—victims as Geoff and I were of 'itchy feet'. They then decided to spend some time in *Melbourne*, and rented a flat close by. Geoff and Ted enjoyed a weekly night out at local pubs to drink a few beers—though ordering a 'midi' or 'pot' (10 oz) rather than an English 'pint'!

Christmas was approaching once again. We still found it strange to celebrate Christmas in the summer-time, remembering the cold, wet—but not often snowy—Christmases we had spent in England. It was cooler here than in *Perth*, and much more comfortable—although *Melbourne* does have a reputation of erratic weather— sometimes producing four seasons in a single day. Mostly though, summers in *Melbourne* were warm and dry, and we did appreciate being able to plan a picnic or barbecue without the threat of bad weather. What was also different was that Christmas in Australia also covers the summer break, with schools and businesses, particularly factories, closing for three weeks, giving a long break over Christmas, the New Year and mid-summer—therefore making it a long year in-between, with no substantial holiday to break it up.

Olive's sister and her family (from Leeds) lived in *Ferntree Gully*, a suburb twenty miles from the city, and she kindly invited the two of us, along with Olive and Ted, to join them for the day. Christmas dinner was the traditional roast turkey (eaten cold), with salad instead of hot vegetables. We loved the variety of fresh salad ingredients available, and enjoyed our first taste of capsicums (peppers). We had a lovely time with all the family, especially seeing what life could be like once we settled down and hopefully had a family of our own. Our New Year's resolution for 1970 was to work hard and save towards that end.

15

Trip to Sydney

1970 was a very busy and eventful year for us. We were determined to work and save hard for our future, especially now that we had decided that Melbourne was the place where we wanted to settle, but we still wanted to see more of Australia, and managed to fit in a few enjoyable events and trips.

Geoff's 25th birthday was in February, and some friends came to the flat to celebrate it with us. I bought Geoff a *Rolling Stones* LP—'Let it Bleed'—even though we had no record player! We had to borrow one from our friends Ted and Olive until we could buy one of our own. We soon added to our vinyl collection with Tom Jones's '*Green, Green Grass of Home*' for me, and later, '*Bridge Over Troubled Water*' by Simon and Garfunkel.

Later that month our nephew Michael was born—my sister Pat's third baby, and I was sad not to be there to cuddle him. I sent a parcel with some hand-knitted garments, and a lovely *Onkaparinga* baby blanket, but was sorry that

I couldn't deliver it in person. We were missing quite a few family and friends' special occasions back in the UK, including weddings and births, and one friend from *Kemptons* asked me to be a godmother by proxy to her new baby daughter. I agreed, but it was strange to do this all by correspondence (no Skype or iChat in those days). I'm sorry to say that I lost touch with them with our frequent changes of address over the next few years.

One of the English women I met at work had moved to *Sydney* in *New South Wales* at the end of 1969 with her husband and three children, and we kept in touch. They invited us to visit, and we took them up on their offer over the ANZAC (*Australian and New Zealand Army Corps*) long weekend in April. We booked coach tickets, but little did we know how long the journey would be, especially as we would be calling at *Canberra* in the *Australian Capital Territory* on the way. The distance covered was approximately 590 miles, and it took us 16 hours! The bus never travelled faster than 40mph, even on the open highways, due to speed restrictions. It was very tiring, and all we can remember of our brief stop in *Canberra*—the capital city of Australia—is that we added to our music collection by buying another LP—'Nat King Cole Sings 24 of his

Greatest Hits'! This is definitely a trip that should be undertaken at leisure to appreciate the sheer vastness and beauty of *Victoria* and *New South Wales*, with maybe a trip to the *Snowy Mountains* included.

Sandra on ferry in Sydney harbour, approaching Opera House

Eventually we arrived in *Sydney* and were met by our friends. They were buying a house in an elevated position, with distant views of *Sydney Harbour.* We took a ferry trip across the water to *Sydney*'s vibrant city centre, passing the impressive *Sydney Harbour Bridge* (completed in 1932) and the famous *Opera House*—still under construction. It's design was much maligned at the time, with Prince Charles saying it looked "like snails mating", but it is now an iconic structure, recognised world-wide. We walked around *Sydney*'s waterfront area, and loved the two-storey Victorian terrace houses, with their verandahs and lace-patterned wrought-iron balustrades.

Geoff and I were keen to see *King's Cross—Sydney*'s answer to *Soho* in *London*—and so in the evening we took a stroll along *Victoria Street* and *Darlinghurst Road*, encompassing the infamous 'red light' district. The streets were bustling, with prostitutes, potential customers and many inquisitive tourists like ourselves, and music blaring out from the many cafés and pubs. As we sauntered along taking in all the colourful sights and sounds, Geoff was surprised to see a familiar face pass by. He called out and the man turned round—it was an old drinking buddy Paul, who Geoff had last seen in *The Royal Oak* pub in Leicester on Paul's 21st birthday four years previously. It was an amazing coincidence, as we had travelled up from *Melbourne* and he had flown down from *Brisbane*, only for us to meet in notorious *King's Cross*! (It was our only visit—and his too, I'm sure).

We had really enjoyed our short break in *Sydney*, but couldn't face the long journey home by coach, so enquired about an alternative at the bus depot. We were really pleased to find that we could exchange our tickets, at a small supplement, and fly back by *Ansett Airlines*, taking less than two hours. We said good-bye to our friends and returned home. We kept in touch with them for a while, but unfortunately, when their marriage broke down, our correspondence ceased too.

In July that year we had our first—and only—chance to go skiing—not something we ever expected to do when moving to live in Australia—Canada, yes, but Australia . . . . ?! It was winter-time, and we were surprised to hear that *Victoria* had many snowfields, including *Mount Buller*, *Mount Hotham* and *Mount Buffalo*. *ESGM's Social Club* had arranged a weekend at *Falls Creek*, another snowfield, four hours drive from *Melbourne*. The weather report was promising, with lots of snow falling over the mountains, and Geoff and I were looking forward to our first attempts at this winter sport. A group of thirty workers and family and friends made the journey in a convoy of several cars and vans. We travelled with a colleague of mine John and his fiancée Gwyn, arriving in the early afternoon. The resort of *Falls Creek* looked so picturesque when we arrived, with deep snow covering the road and trees, and ski lodges looking just like those we had seen pictures of in Switzerland. We were shown to our rooms in one large chalet, and gathered together to get instructions for the next day. Early the next morning we were all keen to get started—not all of us were first-timers—but everyone had great expectations of a fun week-end. We couldn't believe it when we were told that, although there had been heavy snowfalls, there had also been a lot of rain, making it unsafe to ski! We were so disappointed, and couldn't believe our bad luck. Geoff and I spent the day exploring the small resort, and after returning to the lodge for an evening meal, went out again in the dark. Everywhere looked so wonderful, with lights shining from all the windows. We seemed to be the only ones out in the cold, and we threw snowballs at the windows of our colleagues to entice them out. No-one would join us and so we gave up our attempts, and joined everyone for food and drinks in the warm, and to hear some gossip about several après-ski affairs!

Back in *Melbourne* I decided that I would learn to drive, and booked some lessons. After ten lessons driving around the suburb of *Albert Park* (which since 1996 has been home to the *Australian Grand Prix* circuit), with its lovely gardens, lake and beach frontage, I arranged my driving test. After a few questions, a short drive and a reverse parking manoeuvre, I was given my pass certificate. I was very pleased with myself, and the next Monday, when I had a day off but Geoff was working, I said I would drive him to work and collect him later, giving me some much-needed experience of driving on my own. After a ten-minute drive, I dropped Geoff off on *Glenferrie Road, Hawthorn*, and then turned left into the next street, intending to turn around and drive myself home. Unfortunately I attempted a three-point turn half-way along this narrow street, and made a complete mess of it—getting stuck right in the middle of the street in quite busy early morning traffic. Several impatient drivers tooted their horns, but no-one offered any assistance. I eventually managed to turn the car around, and despite feeling really embarrassed and nervous, was able to drive myself home. It had been a really stressful experience for me, and I never drove again.

Not long afterwards, we had the first of two accidents involving our car. This happened one day when we were returning from a day out—we turned right from *Dandenong Road* into *Orrong Road* and then, still indicating, intended to turn right into the driveway and parking space of our flat. Unfortunately the car driver behind must have thought that Geoff had just left the indicator on and so didn't slow down, and he ran straight into the back of our car. Luckily no-one was hurt, though I did develop a painful neck the next day, which lasted for about a week. We took the driver's details, but later when we tried to contact him for insurance purposes, we found the address he gave us was false. We contacted the police, but they couldn't trace him, and so the cost of repairs, amounting to a few hundred dollars, fell to our insurance company. The junction of *Dandenong Road* and *Orrong Road* was a dangerous corner, and we would often hear the screeching of tyres as we watched television, and would hold our breaths waiting for the sound of impact. In those days it was the policy of car repair firms to pay for information of crashes in the hope of being the first on the spot to procure the work. We had a couple of representatives of these companies calling at our flat to leave their cards, as it was known as a black spot for road traffic accidents.

The second incident resulted in our car almost becoming a write-off. Fortunately this time we were not in the car—it was parked in the street between other cars outside a block of flats in *Brunswick*. We were playing cards and having a drink with friends after the men had been playing a game of squash. We heard a couple of loud 'booms', and a friend's brother, who lived in another of the flats, knocked on the door and told us that there had been a big smash involving several cars in the street. Geoff said: "I bet one of them is ours." He was right—a car had hit the back of the last car in a line of six, and ours was in the middle! All the cars were crumpled together—ours looked like the middle section of a concertina! The repair companies were out in force—almost fighting to get the business—and one mechanic asked, "Who's is the Mini?" It was our car, and Geoff replied, "It's not a Mini, it's a Morris 1100." The mechanic gave him a withering look and said, "It's a Mini now"!

Once again our insurance company had to pay for the repairs, which were quite extensive, but the car came back better than before—even the interior light, which wasn't working before the crash, had been repaired! We decided after this that, as we could both get to work easily by tram and the car was becoming more expensive to run, we would manage without one for a while, and we put it up for sale. It was bought by a Greek family living nearby, and we all celebrated the transaction with a glass or two of ouzo!

16

Special Visitor

Squash was a new sport for Geoff, and he really enjoyed a weekly game with Dave, Oscar and Oscar's brother at *Brunswick Sports Centre.* After one particularly exhausting game he couldn't wait for a refreshing shower, and in his hurry to cool off he mistook the signs to the changing rooms and showers, and to his horror, looked up to see several naked women soaping themselves in adjoining showers, while chatting to each other. Fortunately for Geoff they had their backs to him, so had no idea he was there, but he says he has never made such a speedy turnaround as he did that day! He rushed out with his cheeks red with embarrassment, much to the amusement of the two female receptionists!

We both signed on as blood donors around this time at the *Red Cross Blood Centre* in *Flinders Street*—something we had started while in the UK. We continued this for many years in Australia and back in the UK, giving numerous donations between us—hopefully helping to save some lives over that time. We know that Geoff had definitely saved one life in the UK when he was only 17—before we met. One day a young girl of 12 who lived on the other side of *Stephenson Drive,* came rushing over to Geoff who was in the front garden mending a puncture in his bike's front tyre. She shouted for him to come quickly back to her house, as her mother had her head in the gas oven! Geoff went back with her and the woman, aged around 40, was lying on the kitchen floor with her head on a cushion inside the oven, which was on, but unlit. Geoff switched off the oven, opened the back door to let out the noxious fumes, and grabbed her by the ankles, pulling her onto the kitchen floor. She wasn't very appreciative, and told him to "**** off"—so he just left her with her daughter and went home. He never told anyone about this incident at the time, and only told me some years later, but he saw this neighbour on many occasions afterwards—in the street and in the nearby *Newfoundpool Working Mens Club*, so we know that she survived, and in fact, lived into old age.

Geoff's laid-back attitude was also much in evidence when we went camping in the bush one week-end with Dave, Anne, Ted and Olive. The area was near *Ballarat*, 100km (62 miles) north-east of *Melbourne*. Dave and Ted had shotguns with them, though I have no idea what they were expecting to shoot—maybe some rabbits—or a stray kangaroo? We put up our three tents in a clearing, ate barbecued sausages and steak and drank beer and billy tea (we really felt like Aussies now!), before preparing for bed. Once the sun went down there was total darkness under the eucalyptus trees, and we could hear the cicadas serenading us from amongst the ferns and bracken, so we retired to our respective tents. Dave and Ted slept fully clothed, holding onto their guns—goodness knows what they thought might attack in the night—there are no dangerous animals in the Australian bush—apart from snakes, which might slither into our sleeping bags—or poisonous spiders! Geoff, as usual, stripped down to his birthday suit, and zipped himself into his sleeping bag, next to me in mine. The next morning he was well rested and cheerful, and asked the others "Did you sleep OK?" "No", they grumbled, "You kept us awake with your snoring"! I had slept well, being quite used to Geoff's nocturnal noises.

One trek through the bush had uncomfortable consequences for me. Dave, a very tall man, waded through a small billabong and called out, "Come on in, it's not deep." Not thinking I—all 5 feet nothing of me—followed him in, sinking up to my armpits! I was quickly rescued, but something nasty lurking in the deep had taken a nip at me, and the next day I had a very large swelling on the left side of my bottom!

Meanwhile we were doing our best to save for a deposit on a property, but inflation was soaring at this time (as it was worldwide), with prices rising each week above the amount we could save. We hoped to buy a new house (bungalow), and the popular option for first-time buyers at the time was to buy a block of land, and to have a chosen design of home built onto the block by contractors. A favourite week-end outing for us was to visit a 'show home' on a housing development, which had some homes already built and some vacant blocks, with the 'show home' set up with fixtures and fittings and fully furnished, to give an idea of how wonderful they could look with the right decor. These new building projects tended to be in the outer suburbs, and we would visit one on Saturday or Sunday mornings, stop at a *Kentucky Fried Chicken* restaurant for lunch (served with mashed potatoes and spicy gravy—delicious!), and then drive on to another location in the afternoon. We had looked at ready-built houses in the inner suburbs, but they were expensive, and so another option we considered was a 'villa unit'—which were small one or two-bedroomed bungalows, sometimes semi-detached, or four to six units built on a small block, with limited outdoor space or garden.

Our friends Dot and Jim had put a deposit on a block of land at *Chirnside Park* near *Lilydale*, 33 km (21 miles) east of *Melbourne*. This division of the original huge estate encompassed a two-storey homestead, country club and golf course, and new areas of land had become available as building blocks. We drove out with Dot and Jim to see their quarter-acre block on this estate, and thought it was a lovely location. It seemed a good investment, and a way to get us started on course for our own home, so Geoff and I checked out the remaining available plots. We settled on one overlooking the golf course, and put down a deposit, hoping to pay it off in two or three years, and to have enough money saved to build our dream home there soon afterwards.

This year was a particularly busy and memorable one for us, but for *Melbourne* itself there was an unforgettable disaster—the collapse of the *Westgate Bridge*. This bridge had been under construction for two years—built to span the *Yarra River* to link the city and the western suburbs, and out to the city of *Geelong*, 80 km (50 miles) to the south-west. In October 1970 a central section of the bridge fell into the river below, killing 35 construction workers and injuring many others. Work was stopped on the bridge while investigations were undertaken, and construction resumed in 1972. The bridge was finally completed in 1978, and is now a very busy highway in and out of the city. Unfortunately, as in similar constructions, there have been many suicides from the bridge since, but measures have been taken to minimise these, such as the erection of concrete barriers. This was another shocking and unforgettable catastrophe which occurred during our years in Australia.

Later that year we had a lovely surprise in the post. My mum wrote to say that she was coming for a holiday over Christmas and the New Year. It wouldn't be a long visit as she was still working, but we were really looking forward to seeing her, and to showing her around *Melbourne* and introducing her to our friends. She and my sister Pat had joined a 'Family and Friends of Migrants' group which met at the *Belgrave Working Mens Club* in Leicester, and they attended monthly meetings there. The fare from the UK to Australia was still quite prohibitive, but the organisers arranged group bookings at a slightly reduced rate. At the time, having come out to Australia on a leisurely sea cruise, we didn't appreciate what a gruelling journey the 12,000-mile flight could be, which included not only around 22 hours flying time, but also several hours travelling to, and waiting at, airports, with sometimes several hours spent in-between flights. We were so pleased that my mum was travelling with friends, as, being deaf and just 4 feet 10 inches in height, she could so easily have been lost in the crowds!

She was very lucky not to have been detained in Customs though, as one item in her hand luggage could definitely have been described as an offensive weapon. She had asked in advance what she could get Geoff for a Christmas present, and he said he would like a torque wrench, as he had few tools at the time. This is a solid steel bar 16.5" (42cm) long and 1.5" (3cm) in diameter. She had just wrapped it in some festive Christmas paper, and packed it amongst her clothes!

I was excited about my mum's visit, and we made plans to make it a holiday she wouldn't forget. Luckily we had the small spare bedroom, and so prepared that for her. We bought a 5-feet tall artificial Christmas tree, and decorated that and the flat, and wondered what she would make of a hot, sunny Christmas, after leaving behind the cold, damp weather in Leicester. We wanted to help with the cost of her air fare, and as we were now paying for two blocks of land, we decided to sell the land in *Perth.* Unfortunately it wasn't that easy—as part of a syndicate we thought they would buy it back, but we were told that it was up to us to sell it. We put things in motion, but this didn't help us in the short term. Nevertheless, we managed to send mum £100 towards her £700 fare.

I couldn't wait to see my mum, as we had some exciting news of our own for her—I was pregnant! I wanted her to be the first to know, so I didn't mention it at work and we didn't tell any of our friends. It was hard to keep our happy secret—I bought a pretty cotton maternity dress with purple and white flowers and a big white collar, and I sewed up the front pleat temporarily, hoping to disguise my blossoming figure. The first time I wore it our friend Dot said, "That dress makes you look pregnant"! I still didn't tell her our news, and was relieved when it was time to collect my mum from the airport, so I could tell her and then the rest of our family, colleagues and friends. She looked none the worse for her long flight, but did have to take off a few layers of clothes as she emerged into the 90°F heat. We were soon home in the relative coolness of our flat, and I spilled out the news of our expected baby. My mum, a woman of few words, said: "I thought you'd put on some weight"!

17

Fun times in Melbourne & Victoria

It was lovely to have my mum with us over the festive period, and we started the celebrations off with a small party in our flat with a few friends. Mum loved her first experience of a warm, sunny Christmas—even the hotter days with temperatures over 90°F didn't seem to bother her. She was very impressed with the large lemon tree in the garden at the rear of the flat, and enjoyed a slice or two of lemon in a nice cold orange juice or gin and tonic! I didn't tell her at the time of the Aussie custom of the men 'watering' these lemon trees after a few pints of the amber nectar!

Even without a car we were able to take her sight-seeing around the city, starting with the *Shrine of Remembrance* on *St Kilda Road* with its fabulous views, and the nearby *Botanical Gardens*—mum was fascinated by the native black swans on the lake. Close by were the *King's Domain Gardens*, with the *Sidney Myer Music Bowl*—from which open-air music concerts are held all year, culminating in 'Carols by Candlelight' at Christmas. There is a covered awning for the performers, and seating in the open, with space all around for those choosing to picnic on the grassy slopes. And of course, we couldn't miss out a visit to *Captain Cook's cottage* in *Fitzroy Gardens,* and *Melbourne Zoo.*

Mum also enjoyed an outing to the *Harold Holt Memorial Pool*, and although she had never learnt to swim, she had fun splashing about in the sunshine and sharing a picnic by the side of the pool afterwards. This was not our first experience of open-air swimming—I remember trips to the *Lido* open-air pool in Leicester when we were children, and I'm sure the sun was shining— though that might just be memories of long-gone school summer holidays, when the sun always seemed to shine! Dave and Anne joined us on a trip to *Black Rock* beach, 18km south-east of Melbourne. Mum may not have been able to swim, but she cut quite a figure posing in her two-piece black swimsuit on the hot sands!

Mum on Black Rock beach, January 1977

An Australian friend at work invited all three of us to an Aussie-style barbecue, with mum as the guest of honour. It was very kind of her, and we were really looking forward to it. Geoff had finished work that day for his three-week summer break, and had been paid his wages, including holiday pay. It was all in cash and we had no time to get to the bank, so rather than leave it in an empty flat, I put all our money into my purse, which I then put into a pretty black beaded bag, with my powder compact and lipstick. We all then walked to the nearest public telephone box and I rang for a taxi, which picked us up there a few minutes later. We arrived at the party and were made very welcome, but as soon as the taxi drew away I realised I didn't have my handbag. Our friend rang the taxi firm for us immediately, but was told it hadn't been handed in. We then contacted the police and they checked the telephone box for us, but my handbag was nowhere to be seen. This was quite a blow to our finances, and left us without access to any cash over the Christmas/New Year break— no convenient cash/credit cards or ATMs in those days!

Once the banks opened again in the new year (1971) we were able to withdraw some cash, and we hired a car (a *Renault 8*—Geoff was not impressed) for the next week so that we could take my mum further afield to experience more of the delights of the State of *Victoria*. The first place we took her to see was our block of land at *Chirnside Park*, to show her where we might be living when she came out on her next visit—she was duly impressed.

Just one hour's drive north-east of Melbourne is the *Healesville Sanctuary*. This 70 acres of bushland in the *Yarra Valley* is a great place to see Australian wildlife in natural surroundings, including *kangaroos*, *koalas*, *wombats*, *dingoes* and *birds of prey*. There is also a chance to get a close-up of the strange-looking *duck-billed platypus*—this Sanctuary was the first place to oversee the breeding of a platypus in captivity in 1943. Our overwhelming memory of the day though involved the *emus*, which were running about freely in the picnic areas. My mum was just about to tuck into a cheese sandwich when a beady-eyed emu approached from behind and made a snatch at her lunch. She was so surprised she started to run, with the emu in hot pursuit! It wasn't until she threw the food into the air that he was diverted from his course. I'm afraid Geoff and I weren't much help, as we were doubled up with laughter!

Mum, Geoff and a hungry emu!

One attraction we couldn't wait to visit was the newly-built *Sovereign Hill* open-air museum in *Ballarat,* a one-and-a-half hour's drive west of *Melbourne*. It was built to recreate *Ballarat* in the 1850s, at the height of the *Gold Rush*, and was where the famous 'Welcome' nugget of gold was found by a group of Cornish miners in 1858, weighing 69kg—worth around US$43 million today.

Ballarat was also the site of the infamous *Eureka Stockade* rebellion of 1854. The miners, or 'diggers' as they were commonly called, were protesting against the cost of licences. These fees, or taxes, had to be paid regardless of whether any gold was recovered from individual 'claims', and were very unpopular. Tempers were also inflamed by a murder and subsequent burning of a hotel, and the arrest of three miners. Meetings were held to demand the release of these men, and also a decision was made to burn the hated licences in protest. The resulting fight at the *Stockade* barricades between the diggers and police and government troops resulted in the death of 22 diggers and five police troopers. The diggers arrested were later acquitted and a commission into their complaints resulted in votes for miners and a reduction in the cost of licences. The *Southern Cross* (Eureka) flag, which was flown at this rebellion remains an Aussie symbol of protest again injustice.

The replica mining town consists of *Main Street*, with shops including a bakery, apothecary, blacksmiths and photography studio—where visitors can dress in period costume for souvenir snaps, and a bank and post office. Surrounding *Main Street* are tents containing all the essential equipment the miners would need while living and working the gold diggings, and even two small mines to show the harsh working conditions for these men, often with no reward. Running through the centre of the complex is a winding creek, and one of the highlights of our visit was being able to 'pan' for gold in the gently flowing stream. Unfortunately we found no glistening nuggets of gold in our metal plates!

My mum's holiday was coming to a close, and we were sad to see her go home. Dave and Ann took us to the airport to see her on her way. We watched until the BOAC 707 was out of sight. Of course she was looking forward to seeing my two sisters and her three grandchildren again, and she did have to get back to her job in the laundry at *Glenfield Hospital*—only five more years to retirement (she had celebrated her 55th birthday with us in December). She had plenty of photos and souvenirs to share with family and friends, and we hoped this might encourage more visitors to come 'down under'. We looked forward to seeing her again after she retired and could spend longer with us, especially as she would have at least one grandchild on this side of the world on her next visit!

18

New arrival

My pregnancy was progressing very well, with no complications. Our GP was an older, old-fashioned doctor, who had a no-nonsense approach to medicine—and childbirth in particular. After confirming my pregnancy, I was given a prescription for iron tablets, and monthly check-ups at the surgery were arranged (no midwives were involved in the lead-up to the birth). Dr Zacharin would be delivering our baby in hospital, and he pencilled in a due date of 1st July.

Australia has a basic primary health service to supply urgent medical needs, but many people living there take out health insurance to cover private doctors visits, hospital admissions and treatment. Geoff was paying for family health insurance to the HBA (Hospital Benefits Association)—the payments were deducted from his wages weekly, and at the time the amount was probably the equivalent cost of National Insurance contributions taken from wages in the UK. This insurance did give us private health cover though, and we were able to book me into *St Francis*

Xavier Cabrini Hospital in *Malvern* for the birth of our first child.

Meanwhile I was still working in the city—travelling there and back by tram. I was feeling really well with no morning sickness, thank goodness, and just getting bigger and rounder day by day. A friend in the office lent me two maternity dresses in a pinafore style, and I wore these constantly with different blouses. I also bought a small pram and a large wooden cot from her, as her family was complete. All my colleagues were kind and helpful, and I sailed through my pregnancy—the only time off work being an hour here and there for my check-up appointments. My boss even called me into his office one day and said, "My wife says that pregnant women can suffer from swollen ankles and aching backs, and if you need to take time off, that's fine"! He also said later that he regretted not taking up a bet with another (male) employee that I would need to finish work before the date I had given—the end of May (a month before my due date), because I left exactly on the date I had planned. I don't know how much money he would have won if he had taken up the bet, but it just proved the point that Aussies will bet on anything!

We received some lovely parcels from our families in England for our baby-to-be, including a pack of terry nappies from my mum, and a parcel of cute baby clothes from my sister Pat. Unfortunately, instead of sending the parcel to 364 *Dandenong Road*, she addressed it as number 264, which happened to be a large cemetery! Thankfully we called into the P.O. in the city, and were able to retrieve the parcel. So, added to all the matinee coats I had been knitting, our baby would be cosy and warm after his/her arrival sometime in the Melbourne winter of 1971.

Although our flat in *East St Kilda* would accommodate the new arrival, we didn't really want to spend another winter in the chilly, damp atmosphere, especially with a baby, and so decided to look for somewhere more suitable. When mentioning this at work, yet again an Aussie colleague came to the rescue. John, a senior clerk, said that his mother had a rental property available in the suburb of *East Malvern*. Mrs Allen lived in a lovely two-storey house backing onto *Central Park* in *Malvern*, and also owned two shops on *Burke Road*, which she rented out—one was being run as an estate agency and the other a milk bar, the latter shop being owned and run by Mrs Allen and her husband for many years until his death.

The property John described to us was a detached single-storey weatherboard house with two bedrooms in *Ardrie Road*, just a short drive away on the opposite side of *Dandenong*

Road, and sounded ideal. When we went to view it we loved the area—it was a pretty tree-lined street, with the entrance to *Ardrie Park* just a few houses away, but also just around the corner from *Waverley Road*, with small local shops, and the convenient trams into the city and out to the surrounding suburbs.

So we were on the move again, but only a short distance, and we hoped to stay put for longer this time. Most of the houses in the street were small weatherboard 'bungalows', with a few feet separating each one, but there were also some larger brick residences. We moved into No 40 with our few possessions on a lovely sunny day, and immediately felt at home. Although the properties were privately owned and single-storey, *Ardrie Road* was reminiscent of the small streets of terraced houses I knew from childhood, with close neighbours, some of whom became good friends over the next few years. Our new home had a small front garden, and the house had a wooden verandah. The front door opened onto a hallway, with two bedrooms one behind the other on the left, leading into a square sitting room, and beyond that a compact kitchen and bathroom. There was a small garden at the back, mostly lawn, with a rotary clothes drier in the centre—so everything we needed for this new stage in our lives.

We were still without a car, but had some nice days out with friends. One Sunday, when I was nearly eight months pregnant, we went with our friends George and Sylvia to *Phillip Island*—located 140km (87m) south-east of *Melbourne*. The island measures 39 square miles, and is connected from the mainland town of *San Remo* to *Newhaven* on the island by a bridge. It's a beautiful place, and very popular with tourists from the rest of Australia and overseas. Beside the farmland with grazing *sheep* and *cattle*, the wildlife includes *wallabies* and *kangaroos*, and *fur seals* off the western coast. There is an abundant variety of birds too—most famously the population of *Little (Fairy) Penguins*. These can be seen at dusk coming ashore and waddling up the beach to reach their burrows—seemingly oblivious of the crowds of fascinated tourists just inches away. There is also good surfing, and the island is the venue for rock festivals, and also car racing and the *Australian Motorcycle Grand Prix*.

Geoff offered to drive the almost 4-hours return trip, as George wasn't the best at concentrating on long drives—looking over his shoulder to talk to passengers in the back while travelling at speed. His car was a red *Ford Cortina*, which he had recently bought after trading in an old wooden-panelled *Morris Minor* 'Traveller'. He had brought this over by ship a few years previously, and it turned quite a few heads when he drove it around *Melbourne*. We had a lovely day on *Phillip Island*, though I was quite heavily pregnant now, and found it hard to walk too far. We left before dusk, so didn't get to see the 'Penguin Parade', but promised ourselves we'd visit again soon.

At the end of May, as arranged, I finished working in the city. In those days there really wasn't such a thing as 'maternity leave', with the prospect of returning to the same job after a few weeks or months—women left work to have their babies, and looked for a new position when or if they were ready to resume paid employment. The firm gave me a leaving party, and presented me with a baby bath set in sunny yellow (no way of knowing the sex of the baby then). I said goodbye and promised to let them know as soon as our baby was born—hopefully in the not-too-distant future!

Once I had finished work, the time dragged. Although I tried to keep busy, the days were long, with Geoff working 10-12 hour shifts, and me not yet having met any of our close neighbours. I was keeping well, having regular check-ups, and getting bigger by the hour. One evening we went to the nearby *Belgrave Cinema* to see 'Butch Cassidy and the Sundance Kid', starring Paul Newman and Robert Redford. Geoff bought our tickets and as we entered the auditorium, the male usher pointed at my stomach and asked: "You're not going to have that in here, are you?"! It was a great film, and luckily the excitement of it didn't precipitate an early labour!

July 1st dawned bright and cool (it was winter in *Melbourne*), but with no sign of our baby's imminent arrival. Pat in England was hoping to hear the good news before she and her family set off on their annual summer holiday to their caravan in *Mablethorpe, Lincs.*

We still had no telephones between us, and Geoff had promised to send telegrams with the glad tidings. So we all waited—and waited. Two weeks later Dr Zacharin decided it was time our baby made an appearance, and I was admitted to hospital on the evening of 14th July to be induced. I was settled into a room with three other women who had recently had their babies—it was a busy time of year for the maternity unit in *Cabrini Hospital*, and I felt a bit of a fraud walking about, waiting for things to get started.

Early the next morning, with some medical encouragement, my labour was under way. Geoff came in to see me, but as things were progressing slowly, he went off to a nearby café on *Glenferrie Road* for breakfast. He returned and spent some time with me, and some time with other anxious fathers-to-be in the waiting room, then went back to the same café for lunch. He rang the hospital before returning and was told to come in as it wouldn't be long now—but our baby was not going to be rushed. Finally, at 6.40pm on 15th July, our son was born, weighing a healthy 8lb 14oz. Unfortunately it was a forceps delivery, so quite traumatic for us both. When he was shown to me he had one bloodshot eye and a small cut above it, but I felt that I recognised him because he was so like Geoff in the photographs I had seen of him as an infant. As it had been a difficult birth I wasn't allowed to hold him, and he was whisked off to the nursery, while I went into theatre for some after care. Some time later, after around ten hours of labour and an hour or so in surgery, I was on a trolley being wheeled back to my room, when we passed several doctors scrubbing up ready for the next arrivals. One of them (male) turned around to me with a big grin and said: "That wasn't too bad, was it?"!!

19

Joy and sorrow

We called our new son Rodney—a popular name in Australia at the time. He was kept in the nursery along with the other babies, and at visiting times the new fathers, families and friends congregated at the big windows to see the new arrivals. The nurses held up the babies, swaddled in blankets, for everyone to admire. One visitor said, "That's a big, handsome baby." "He's mine," said Geoff proudly.

Geoff had sent off the telegrams with our good news as promised to our families in England, who were all now back from their annual summer holidays. My sister used a neighbour's telephone to ring the hospital (calls had to be booked ahead in those days, especially at Christmas-time, and were very expensive). Luckily it was visiting time, and Geoff was able to take the call—I wasn't allowed out of bed, and the only telephone was in reception. She was thrilled for us, but like me, would have loved to give her new nephew a cuddle. The first few days were an emotional time, as I couldn't have my baby at the end of my bed like the other mums or feed him, as I was told he needed time to recover from his difficult birth. I did get out of bed to visit the nursery, but could only stand by his crib and watch him sleeping. Eventually he was brought to me for feeding, but I had difficulty breastfeeding, as he had been bottle fed initially. I was quite upset, but determined to persevere.

I was in hospital for ten days, and one of my first visitors was our landlady Mrs Allen. She explained to the staff that I had no close family in Australia, and they were happy to let her in to see me outside visiting hours. She was such a kind lady, and insisted that Geoff came to her house every evening for dinner while I was in hospital. Other visitors were our friends, Jim and Dot, and Dave and Anne. It was sad not to have close family visitors, but they all sent their congratulations by post. *Cabrini Hospital* arranged for all new babies to have photographs taken in their cribs, so we were able to send lovely pictures of Rodney aged just four days old to our families so far away.

The day to take our new baby home finally arrived. Geoff came in a taxi to collect us, but before he could take his wife and new son home he had to call into the office to settle our account. (The first thing he did when we arrived home was to go out again to the *HBA* office to claim back the amount, then he took the money to the bank to put it into our account to cover the cheque!) We waved goodbye to the wonderful staff of *St Francis Xavier Cabrini Hospital*, with the advice to buy a dummy (pacifier) for our new baby on the way home!

Some things we hadn't expected to have to buy were feeding bottles and sterilising equipment (a large steel pan in which to boil the glass bottles and teats), and also tins of *Carnation* milk, which, combined with boiled water, was the formula used in the hospital to feed the new-borns. I was feeding Rodney myself, but also giving him some formula after each feed to satisfy his huge appetite, so it was quite tiring. Rodney was thriving, but I was not recovering as quickly as I thought I should so, having no-one close to discuss my problems with, I rang Dr Zacharin from the telephone box at the end of the street. I was quite upset when trying to explain my symptoms and difficulties to him and burst into tears, at which point he told me to pull myself together and ring him again when I was more composed. Needless to say, I never rang back. Fortunately I was taking Rodney for his check-ups at the baby clinic, and the nurse there was very understanding. She listened to my problems, and reassured me that I was doing fine, and that Rodney was healthy and progressing well. He rewarded her kindness by directing a stream of water directly at her filing cabinets when she took off his nappy to weigh him! (That is an important lesson to learn with baby boys—never take off a nappy within reach of anything valuable or precious—our record collection received quite a drenching in one unguarded moment!)

Now that I had my baby, and was taking him out in his pram to the local shops, I began to meet our neighbours. Stopping to admire a new baby is a great way to introduce yourself, and the first person I met this way was Pat, who went on to become a very good friend. She was pregnant herself, with just a few weeks to go. She lived with her husband Fred in a four-bedroomed brick house opposite, with their four daughters, Jennifer 10, Diane 8, Chrissie, 6 and Barbie, 4. It was lovely to have someone to talk to about babies—especially such an experienced mum—and after her son Graeme was born three months later, our boys went on to become great friends.

The next neighbour I met on a trip to the shops was Flo, who was English from Chorley in Lancashire, and married to Ray, an Australian. They lived a few houses away on the same side of the road, and had a daughter Sarah, who was just a few months old. I was admiring Sarah in her pram, when Flo said she was expecting again, and on seeing my expression (I couldn't imagine having two babies so close together, as I was struggling coping with one), she said she was pleased, and had planned it that way. Flo said she knew I came from Leicester in the Midlands when I complained that I hadn't even had time to "mash" (brew) some tea! Flo had emigrated to Australia, like us, but had travelled over on her own, sailing on the *Castel Felice* in 1968 and later married a true-blue Aussie, Ray. About six months after I met her she had a boy (I think I had started a trend), and called him Bruce—a good Aussie name. Flo and Ray had another boy, Andrew some years later after moving out to *Rosebud*, a lovely seaside town on the *Mornington Peninsula*, 75km (46m) south-east of Melbourne, which was very popular with tourists and campers for its sandy beaches and shallow waters.

To complete the circle (or square?), an Australian couple, Rhyll and Pete, who were renting a weatherboard house next to Pat and Fred (who owned it), had the first of three sons, Robert (Bob), followed over the next few years by Benjamin (Ben) and Barnaby (Barny). These boys all grew up to be giants—the shortest, Bob, reaching a height of 6' 2", was called "shortarse" by his brothers!

We loved living in Ardrie Road, and with making new friends in the neighbourhood, began to feel very settled. Geoff was still working long shifts though, and I sometimes found it hard to cope with a new baby on my own most of the day. We had no washing machine, so I was washing everything by hand, including nappies. It was winter in Melbourne too, and one particular day I remember having pinned out a line of nappies on the rotary clothes dryer in the garden, then going to the shops, pushing Rodney in his pram and pulling a shopping trolley behind. On the way back to the house it started to rain, and I was close to tears thinking of that line of nappies getting soaked. Some time later Flo said that she had seen me out of her front window, and thought that I now looked very organised and in control. If only she had known! The outcome of this was that we arranged for a nappy service to call weekly to leave me a supply of clean white towelling nappies, and to collect all the soiled ones. This service—in the days before disposables—made a huge difference to me, and I was finally able to settle into a routine and to really enjoy being a new mum.

When Rodney was six weeks old Dave and Anne came over to babysit, to give us a break, and some much-needed time alone together. We set off into the city to see a film at the *Forum* in *Flinders Street*, but I don't remember the film at all—we spent the whole time wondering how Rodney was, and if Dave and Anne were coping. Of course everything was fine when we arrived home, and Rodney had rewarded them by filling his nappy—good practice for the future!

I took him into the city to show him off to my former work colleagues, and to return the dresses to my friend, which I'd had dry-cleaned. It was quite a performance getting him and his pram onto the tram (no hooks on the back here). Rodney was a great hit with the ladies though, and it was nice to have a trip into the city again.

We were very comfortable in the house on *Ardrie Road*, though it was in need of some updating, and Geoff asked Mrs Allen if she would mind if he did some decorating. She was quite happy for him to go ahead, and he started with the second bedroom, painting the ceiling, walls and woodwork. Once this was completed, we moved Rodney from his cradle by our bed to a cot in the newly-decorated room. The plaster on the living room walls was quite cracked and flaky, so Geoff bought some wallpaper in a light beige with a small pattern. He'd had some experience of paper-hanging at home in England, but papering walls was not usual practice in Australian homes. John, our landlady's son, was painting the outside of the house at the time, and was quite sceptical, but he was very impressed with the finished result, so much so that he went out and bought the very same wallpaper for a house he was renovating at the time. Mrs Allen too thought it looked very nice, and I think was pleased that we were making some improvements to her house.

Early in December we had a day out at *Lake Eildon* with Anne and Dave. Eildon is 144km (89 miles) north-east of Melbourne, and is a popular holiday resort. The lake was created by the construction of a new dam in the 1950s, and is surrounded by rolling hills. It is a great venue for watersports, and we had a lovely boat trip across the water.

Another Christmas was fast approaching—much more exciting now that we were a family of three, and I had lots of fun buying toys and treats to celebrate. We had presents from our families overseas to put under our tree too, so I was anticipating a special time with our new baby, and his first Christmas. Mrs Allen invited us all for Christmas lunch, and we were looking forward to spending some time with her and John and John's sister, Judith.

We walked over to Mrs Allen's house on a warm, sunny morning, and were soon enjoying pre-lunch drinks in the garden. We had just been called indoors for lunch when there was a knock at the door. John opened it, and was surprised to see two police officers standing outside. He invited them in and we all looked at them expectantly, never dreaming of the tragic news we were about to hear. Mrs Allen's brother and family were driving to—or returning from—we are not sure which, a holiday in Queensland by car, towing a caravan, and had been involved in a head-on collision with a truck. This was carrying tools and cans of petrol (illegally), which burst into flames. Mrs Allen's brother, his wife, daughter and their dog were all killed, as was the driver of the truck. It was such unexpected and devastating news, and Geoff and I were so shocked that this could happen to such a nice family, especially on Christmas Day. We suggested we should go home to give the family time to get over the shock and to make arrangements, but Mrs Allen insisted we stay for lunch, as she knew we wouldn't have bought in much festive fare. It was a very good meal, but no-one really had much of an appetite, and the conversation was understandably strained. We really didn't know what to say, other than to offer our condolences, and we left early to take Rodney home to play with his new Christmas toys—at five months old he had no idea of the sorrowful events that had just taken place.

20

Work and play

We had paid off our block of land at *Chirnside Park*, but decided to sell it—mainly because we liked living in an inner suburb close to the city, and within easy reach of work for Geoff. We had also seen the large houses that were being built on the development, and thought that the modest dwelling we had in mind would look lost among such grand properties. We made a good profit from the sale and were pleased with the boost to our savings.

1972 was a Leap Year, and my 24th (6th) birthday on 29th February was a quiet affair. With Geoff still working long hours and having a young son, we hadn't made any plans to celebrate. I must admit I was feeling very sorry for myself, and in the evening I lay on the bed, flicking through some magazines, when there was a knock on the front door. Flo and Rhyll, knowing it was a 'special' birthday, had brought me a single, large red *Waratah* flower. They wished me a happy birthday, but couldn't stay as they had to get back to their own young families. I really appreciated the gesture though, and it lifted me out of the doldrums.

I wasn't happy about my post-baby weight, and mentioned to Pat that I wanted to join a slimming club. She had the same problem, and we joined a small group to seek advice and support. We enjoyed the weekly meetings with like-minded women. It was a gradual process, but even though neither of us lost an enormous amount of weight, it did keep us mindful of what we ate, and I especially appreciated the break from routine and the chance to expand my circle of friends. Another group Pat and I joined was a craft circle to learn to crochet. We only got as far as making squares, but it was another enjoyable outing. Pat is a very skilled dressmaker, and her girls especially were always clothed in the prettiest summer dresses. My own particular skill was knitting, and I was never without some knitting needles and wool close by. I found it relaxing, and when I had run out of things to knit for myself, Geoff and Rodney, I knitted for Pat's four girls and Graeme, and also for Flo's children.

Pat and Fred swapped their Holden station wagon for a VW Campervan, and added extra seats to accommodate their large family. The big orange van was a common sight in the neighbourhood, with Pat driving the girls to and from school and to all their after-school activities. She also picked me up for trips to nearby *Chadstone Shopping Centre*. Once every two or three months the *Red Cross* mobile blood donation truck was stationed on the car park there, and we both gave our donations— sometimes before attending our slimming class. This resulted in a modest, but sadly temporary, weight loss!

On Rodney's first birthday in July we had a party for him and his young friends. He had begun walking and looked really cute in a brown zip-up all-in-one suit, sent by his Aunty Ann. People remarked how much he looked like Geoff, with his blonde hair and green eyes. We arranged for a professional photographer to come to take some special photographs to mark the occasion.

Now that my baby had grown into a toddler, I decided to look for a part-time job to have some much-needed time away from the house. I saw an advert for a kitchen assistant at *Evancourt Hospital*, just a short distance away on *Dandenong Road*. The position was only for two hours a day, Monday to Friday, but I was keen to get back into the workforce, even at a small starting salary (every little helps!) I attended an interview, and was introduced to the cook, Wynne. I was offered the job, and arranged to start the next week. The hours were 5pm-7pm, but Geoff didn't get home from work until 6pm. Pat came to the rescue and said she would be happy to look after Rodney for that first hour. It worked out very well—Rodney enjoyed his play dates with his best pal Graeme, and Geoff collected him from Pat's as soon as he arrived home, and later they both came to meet me out of work. My duties in the kitchen were to help prepare the evening meal for the patients and to wash dishes. I enjoyed working with Wynne, an English woman in her early sixties, and we became good friends.

Geoff was a fan of *Joe Cocker*, an English rock/blues singer, who was touring Australia in October 1972. During the latter part of the tour, Joe and six members of his entourage were arrested in Adelaide for possession of marijuana. They were allowed to continue onto Melbourne the next day, but were then charged with assault after a brawl at the *Commodore Chateau Hotel*. The Federal Police gave Joe and his band 48 hours to leave the country, which resulted in an outcry from his many fans in Australia. Geoff and his friend Ron had booked tickets for an evening concert the next day, but as Joe would be on his way back to England then, a midnight concert was arranged for everyone holding tickets. Geoff and Ron attended and said Joe put on a great show. During the performance Geoff remarked to Ron about the strange 'sweet' smell in the air. Ron said, "That's marijuana." So much for the ban—I think everyone attending the concert that night was on a 'high'!

Christmas was quiet and uneventful this year. As Christmas Day fell on a Monday and hospitals never close, I went into work for my designated two hours. I didn't really mind, although it was very hot in the kitchen and the patients, mostly elderly, didn't have much appetite for their special meals. Despite having good friends and neighbours now, I was still missing close family, especially at this time of year, and so Geoff and I decided to take a holiday to England in the summer of 1973. We felt we needed this, not only to see our loved ones and to introduce Rodney to his English relatives, but we also hoped it would help us to decide if we were really committed to staying in Australia for good.

We booked flights on *Singapore Airlines* for late June, to return six weeks later. I thought I might have to give up my job at the hospital, but Pat again came to the rescue. She suggested stepping into my shoes, and working the two hours daily until I returned. It would be a change for her, and Fred would be there to look after their children. We consulted the manager of the hospital and he was in agreement, so that was one problem solved. Pat said that she might not let me have my job back when I returned, but I think six weeks of working in a hospital kitchen was too much like being at home, and she was pleased to hand the task back to me. Pat continued to work at the hospital, but as a Healthcare Assistant (Nursing Aide), with in-house training from the nurses at *Evancourt*. She later underwent formal training to gain qualifications in this field. Geoff's boss wasn't so obliging about his extended leave, and told him that his job may not be waiting for him on his return. Geoff said he would worry about that in six weeks time.

Another thing we thought about before setting off on our long, expensive break was the cost of paying rent for the weeks we would be away. It was essential, of course, to have a home to return to, but we were trying not to make too big a dent in our savings. Unbelievably, Pat and Fred came to our aid once again. They owned another weatherboard property in Ardrie Road and as it would become vacant during our time away, said they would be happy to rent it to us on our return.

Before we accepted their exceptionally kind offer though, we had to tell them of our future plans. Wynne, my friend at *Evancourt Hospital*, was also working as a live-in housekeeper for a man in near-by *Wilmot Street*. This street runs from *Ardrie Park* to *Dandenong Road*, and we had often walked along it, admiring the mix of brick and weatherboard houses, thinking it would be a lovely place to live. Wynne knew the woman who lived with her young son at No 18, and had heard that she was soon to be married and would be putting the house up for sale. Wynne introduced us to her, and we were given a tour of the house. It was a detached cream weatherboard bungalow, with a tiled roof. It had a small front garden, tiled verandah, two bedrooms at the front, a sitting room, bathroom, large dining kitchen and a utility room at the back. There was also a double garage to the side of the house. The large garden at the back of the house had a tree house and a round above-ground swimming pool. As well as the obligatory lemon tree, there was a peach tree, fig tree and two plum trees. We loved the house, and came to an agreement over the price there and then. As the house was not yet up for sale, we made plans to contact the owner as soon as we returned from our trip to discuss the deposit and to organise a mortgage with our bank.

We outlined these plans to Pat and Fred, explaining that we might only need to rent their house for a few weeks after our return, and they were quite happy to let us take it on that basis. We gave our notice to Mrs Allen, and although she was disappointed to lose us as tenants, she wished us well for the future and urged us to keep in touch. So we packed up our belongings, including some furniture, and moved them the short distance to No 46, before setting off for the airport to fly the 12,000 miles to England to introduce Rodney to his family on the other side of the world.

21

Trips to England and Scotland

We were soon on our way to Tullamarine Airport. Although it was a long flight with just a brief stop in Singapore airport to refuel, it took us a lot less time to get 'home'—just a total of 25 hours, compared to the 25 days it had taken us to sail to Australia. The flight was mainly smooth and uneventful, and the airline crew, especially the hostesses in their colourful 'Sarong Kebaya' uniforms, were efficient and attentive. Geoff and I squeezed into our cabin seats in economy class, at first feeling very claustrophobic. Rodney however had a good time running up and down the aisles. The airline food was good, although not to Rodney's taste, but he drank plenty of pineapple juice, so we didn't worry. Alcoholic drinks were served with meals and frequently throughout the flight, so Geoff and I were happy!

Finally we arrived at our destination and after collecting our baggage, passed through to the arrivals lounge. Rodney, who was perched on top of our suitcases on a trolley, nearly fell off in fright when our waiting relatives cheered our arrival. Pat,

Ted and their children and Ted's sister Jose, her husband Tom and son Thomas had come to meet us and to drive us the 100 miles from Heathrow, London to Leicester in the Midlands, where we would be staying with my mum for the next few weeks. After nearly six years, it felt strangely familiar to be back in Leicester—although nothing appeared to have changed, roads seemed narrower and houses smaller. The weather was sunny and around 20°C, not too bad for an English summer, but about the same temperature it had been in Melbourne when we had left in their mid-winter.

It had been a tiring journey, but it was lovely to see all our family again. Rodney was introduced to his great-grandmother (Nana), great-grandfather (Dad), grandmother (Granny Green), great-uncles, uncles, aunts and cousins, all who wanted to hug him and say "hello". He was overwhelmed at first to meet so many new people, but after a good sleep in the box-room at Granny Green's, he was full of beans and loved all the attention.

One of the first excursions we planned was a tour of Scotland. Geoff and I had sailed half-way around the world, but had never crossed the English/Scottish border, so we decided to spend a week of our break exploring the Highlands. Pat and Ted had never been to Scotland either, so agreed to join us. We planned to stay in B & B (bed and breakfast) accommodation along the way, but had no particular route planned. Pat and Ted and their three children, Tony, Sharan and Michael, travelled in their yellow Ford Zephyr (with everything but the kitchen sink packed into the back), and Geoff, Rodney, my mum and I followed in a 1957 blue Austin A35, lent to us by a relative. It was a cute little car, but quite a few people thought it wouldn't make the long journey. In fact, it proved to be very sturdy and reliable—the only problem encountered was when we were on a motorway on the way home, and as I opened the small quarter light window, it broke off and was lost. (We managed to replace this later with one found in a scrapyard).

Our whistle-stop tour began in *Gretna Green*, a village just over the border in the south of Scotland, famous for its 'runaway' weddings since 1754. In England and Wales at that time a young couple could be banned from marrying if they were under 21 and their parents objected (*Lord Hardwickes Marriage Act)*. This did not apply in Scotland, where boys of 14 and girls of 12 could marry, with or without parental consent. Since 1929 the legal age in Scotland has been 16, with or without consent, but in England and Wales the age for marriage is 16 with parental consent and 18 without. Hence under-age couples could travel over the border to marry in Scotland, and Gretna

Green became famous for such 'elopements'. Weddings are performed at *The Old Blacksmith's Shop*, built in 1712, where services are conducted over an anvil. Today *Gretna Green* is one of the world's most popular wedding venues.

We hadn't booked any accommodation ahead, and had to knock on the doors of houses with signs saying "vacancies" in the window. Our first night was spent in a large house, which luckily had room for all nine of us. It had been a tiring day, and we hadn't had time for an evening meal, so Pat, mum and I settled the children into their beds, while Geoff and Ted went out to get fish and chips for us all. They tried to sneak them back to our rooms, but as they were passing the sitting room the landlady came out and said "Don't be shy—bring your food and family in here to eat." She had set out a small supper for all the guests, and we were so embarrassed to take in our pungent, newspaper-wrapped food. We hadn't known about this aspect of Scottish hospitality.

We did a lot of driving in-between stops, taking in all the wonderful Scottish scenery—magnificent mountains and picturesque lochs (lakes). We were following Pat and Ted in their car, and soon became used to their quirky sense of direction—if in doubt, travel two or three times round a 'roundabout' (traffic island) until sure of the way forward. Geoff would stop at a junction and wait to join them once they decided which way to go! Pat would also ask Ted to stop for regular breaks, and if no suitable picnic site was spotted, insisted he stopped at the side of the road, even on busy highways, so that she could brew up a refreshing hot drink for us all on a small primus stove. After setting off again, we usually came across a designated picnic area just minutes later. (To be fair, she was concerned that mum had regular snacks, as she had recently been diagnosed with diabetes). As a result of these frequent breaks, whenever we stopped for any reason, Rodney would get out of our car, take his plastic cup to her and say: "Cup of tea, Aunt Pat?"

We continued our journey north, enjoying the beautiful Scottish landscape. *Loch Lomond* was an impressive sight—particularly as we watched a number of jet fighter plane pilots flying at low altitude from one end to the other (25 miles/39km). One of our overnight stays was on a farm, which was a real treat for us 'townies'. The food was fresh and delicious, and the children loved seeing the cows, sheep and chickens, and especially enjoyed playing with some sheepdog puppies. The farmer even promised to name four of the puppies Tony, Sharan, Michael and Rodney. After a substantial breakfast, we wanted to settle our account with the farmer's wife. She had looked after us so well, but she wouldn't charge anything for the "wee bairns" as she said they hadn't eaten much. We met nothing but kindness from our Scottish hosts, and when enquiring about accommodation for the night, if there was not enough room for all of us in one guesthouse, the owner would telephone around to find somewhere else for the rest of us to stay. One evening when we had arrived fairly late in *Fort William*, we had to stay in separate accommodation, and Geoff and I found a room in a bungalow. Our bedroom had a large picture window with fabulous views overlooking *Loch Linnhe*. Dominating the landscape of *Fort William* is *Ben Nevis*, the highest mountain in the British Isles, and very popular with walkers and climbers. Thousands of intrepid travellers complete the climb (over 4,000 feet) every year, but are warned of the weather conditions, which can change quite dramatically from base to summit.

We didn't have the time—or energy—for any mountain climbing, but we were keen to visit *Loch Ness*, 38 miles (79km) to the north-east of *Fort William*, to see if we could spot *The Loch Ness Monster* which is said to inhabit the deep waters. It took us less than two hours to drive the scenic route to *Loch Ness*, but Rodney was feeling really nauseous and just before we reached our destination, he threw up all over me. My first sight of the Loch was from a crouched position at the lake-side while washing my stained blouse in the icy cold water. *Loch Ness* is 23 miles (36km) long, and very deep (nearly 1,000 feet). There have been many claims of sightings of the 'Monster'—said to be an aquatic creature, a mixture of reptile and amphibian, with a long neck and small head, and a body measuring 6-9 metres in length. There is even some disputed photographic evidence, but the beast is mostly considered a myth. We didn't get a sighting of 'Nessie' during out time by the Loch, but, as I said to the children, "Just because we didn't see her, doesn't mean she's not there"!

We began our journey home, but couldn't leave 'Bonnie Scotland' without a visit to *Edinburgh*, the capital city, situated on the east coast. The iconic *Edinburgh Castle*, home to many Scottish monarchs, including Queen Margaret and Mary Queen of Scots, overlooks the city, and is Scotland's leading tourist attraction. We didn't explore the inside of the Castle, but enjoyed the impressive views over the city from the ramparts. Before leaving *Edinburgh* we visited *Princes Street* for some retail therapy, and bought some lovely gifts and souvenirs before continuing our journey south. We had really enjoyed our trip north of the border, and had covered around 1,000 miles, but now wanted to visit family, friends and places in England before our return to Australia.

22

Home visits

Our first trip was to *Brighton*, 131 miles (210 km) away on England's south coast. This is a lovely seaside town, with many famous landmarks, such as the domed *Royal Pavilion*, a former royal residence, *Brighton Pier*—1,719 feet (524m) long, with an amusement arcade and fairground rides and 'The Lanes', a quaint area of alleyways, with a mixture of antique and jewellery shops alongside modern boutiques and cafés. *Brighton* is only 50 miles from London, easily accessible by road and train, and so is a very popular week-end getaway for the big city workers.

Aunt Kath had married again after the death of her first husband Lawrence (Uncle Lol), and was now living in Scotland Street, *Brighton* with her second husband Ted—an ex-Royal Navy Chief Petty Officer. We took mum with us to visit her sister, and Geoff, mum, Aunt Kath and I enjoyed sitting on the pebbled beach in the sunshine, while Rodney splashed about in the *English Channel.* Seeing mum and Aunt Kath together was like looking at twins. They were born less than two years apart and were both petite—though what they lacked in size they made up for in spirit! Aunt Rose, their much taller older sister, had also re-married after the death of Uncle Fred, and later we drove to Coalville in Leicestershire to say 'hello' to her and to meet her new husband, George.

We couldn't be back in England without calling in to see cousin Iris and her family. Geoff and I had visited them often before we left the country, and Iris and I had kept in touch with letters and cards over the years. They had moved from Leicester to *Farnham*, a market town in Surrey, where Iris and Tommy has bought a newsagents. They were kept very busy running this thriving business, whilst living in a flat above the shop with their children Anne, now 13, and Robert 10, but Iris still found the time to organise a party in our honour. We had a lovely time, with even my mum joining in the dancing, and Iris made a great fuss of us all, especially Rodney. Geoff did make the mistake though of trying to keep up with Tommy in a whiskey-drinking competition. It was no contest—Tommy, a lovely, softly-spoken Irishman—won hands down!

Pat and Ted had bought a small caravan for family holidays, situated on a small site close to the beach at *Mablethorpe* in *Lincolnshire* on the east coast, and Geoff and I borrowed it for a few days—we wanted Rodney to see where we had spent many happy holidays with our families when we were young. *Mablethorpe* is a small seaside town, with sand dunes and safe, sandy beaches for the children. Along the esplanade there is a small funfair, crazy golf game and a kiosk to buy the essential bucket and spade, postcards and 'kiss me quick' hats (only in the UK!) For rainy days there are amusement arcades, souvenir shops, indoor markets and the traditional sweet shops, selling sticks of rock in rainbow colours, humbugs and huge dummies (pacifiers). Rodney love sleeping in the cosy caravan, building sandcastles on the beach and paddling in the sea. My favourite treat had been riding a donkey on the beach—a group of six to eight donkeys would walk up and down the beach constantly with excited toddlers on their backs, but Rodney wasn't keen on them at all—he much preferred building sandcastles on the beach and riding the motorbikes and cars in the arcades. It had been a lovely break for just the three of us, but it was time to head back to Leicester to continue our extended holiday with family and friends.

A place we love to visit in England is *Stratford-upon-Avon* in *Warwickshire*, mostly famous for being the birthplace of *William Shakespeare* (1564-1616). We took Rodney's cousin, young

Geoff with us to keep him company, and after a walk around the shops (they weren't interested in the history and culture of this lovely market town), we sat on the grass by the *River Avon*, eating a picnic lunch and feeding the crumbs to the swans, with the *Swan Theatre* directly behind.

Rodney's second birthday on 15th July was a real family affair. We had a party for him at mum's with his cousins, Tony, Sharan, Michael, Diane, Geoff and Marie, and second cousins Jayne and Simon, Marian and Roy's children. He loved being the centre of attention, and especially all the presents. His Aunt Pat took him to *Stanton*'s newsagents on Fosse Road to buy him some *Matchbox* toy cars to add to his collection. Rodney had a large plastic case to keep all his cars in, and had already amassed over twenty. He knew exactly the ones he already had though, and as Pat held up one at a time from the large selection available, he told her if he already had that particular one. She was amazed that he could remember them so well. Nana gave him £20, which he saved until we returned to Australia, and then chose to spend it on a bright yellow peddle car, which he loved. We sent photos back to his Nana, showing him proudly peddling it along *Ardrie Road.*

Rodney in peddle car—Ardrie Road, August 1973

One of our last trips was to *Abbey Park* with Pat and her children, to give Rodney the chance to play in the paddling pool, and to feed the ducks on the boating lake over the other side of the park. It brought back many good memories for Geoff and me, especially as it was the place we had first met some ten years earlier.

Before leaving England we met up with Geoff's friend Mick and his wife, and had a lovely pub meal. We also visited our friends Rod and his wife Cassandra, who we had kept in touch with, exchanging letters and cards, and later photos of our respective children.

On our last night in England we went to the *Fish and Quart* for a meal with Pat and Ted, Sylvia and her husband Ron, and Ken and Ann. It was a lovely evening, and a special ending to our six-week break. The next morning we set off for *Heathrow* airport on the M1 motorway to begin our long journey back to Melbourne. There was Geoff, Rodney and me, Pat and Ted with Sharan and Michael, and Ken, Ann, Diane, Geoff and Marie—all squeezed into two cars for the journey. (There always seemed to be two cars involved in our travels). It had been a wonderful holiday, and although it had demonstrated to us how important family was, we were excited at the prospect of buying our own house in *Wilmot Street*, and couldn't get back quickly enough to set the wheels in motion.

We heard later that after we had said good-bye to everyone and boarded our flight, they all went up to the viewing platform on the roof to watch our plane depart. There was a garden there too, and a small paddling pool. It was a hot day, and the children had a great time splashing about in the pool after stripping down to their underwear.

Our return flight with *Singapore Airlines* was again fairly uneventful, apart from a worrying episode during our break to refuel in *Singapore* itself. As this would be taking over five hours, all the passengers continuing on to Australia were to be taken to a hotel near the airport, rather than spend the time waiting in the airport lounge. This was a nice surprise, and would give us a chance to see something of *Singapore* itself. We walked down the steps from the plane onto the runway and were met by a blanket of hot, humid air. Just the walk across the tarmac to the airport building made us breathless, and it was a relief to reach the air-conditioned building. We were then all transported by coach to the *Hotel Equatorial,* where we were given our own rooms to leave our luggage and to refresh ourselves.

Singapore is situated in south-east Asia, almost on the equator, and consists of 63 islands. Modern *Singapore* was founded as a trading post for the *East India Company* by *Sir Stamford Raffles* in 1819, and became a sovereign state of Great Britain in 1824. It was occupied by the Japanese in World War II, and gained independence from Britain in 1963. Today it is a leading centre of finance, with a very busy port, and is a very wealthy country. The city itself is crowded, vibrant and busy, with many museums and theatres. There are numerous restaurants, bars and clubs, and endless shops and markets to tempt tourists to part with their cash.

It had been arranged for all the passengers to be taken on a brief tour of the city by coach before returning to the airport, but unfortunately, after taking much-needed showers and some refreshment, Geoff, Rodney and I had missed the coach. We didn't want to lose this opportunity to see the sights, so we ordered a taxi to pick the three of us up and drop us in the city. We spent a lovely hour or so walking about the city centre—Geoff admiring the electronics and cameras, while I swooned over the stunning jewellery displays. It was evening now and cooler, but Rodney was getting tired, and we needed to get back to our hotel. We hailed a taxi, and although the driver didn't speak any English, we told him the name of the hotel, and even showed him a postcard with a picture of it. He nodded and seemed to understand and we trusted that he knew where he was going—how wrong can you be? The hotel was seven miles (11km) from the city centre, and we had given ourselves just enough time to get back there, collect our bags and board the coach back to the airport. We settled into the back of the car for the expected fifteen minute drive, but soon began to regret taking this particular cab. We began to get very anxious when our driver stopped at one, then two, then three hotels around the city, asking each time if this was the one! We were beginning to panic now as it was getting late, so Geoff told the driver to stop, and we quickly jumped out. Geoff flagged down another taxi, and this time the driver spoke

English and drove us directly to the hotel, in the nick of time to join our fellow passengers for our onward journey.

We were so relieved to settle into our seats in the Boeing 707 (no matter how cramped we were), and to complete our journey to Melbourne, our home for the foreseeable future.

23

A home of our own

On our return to Melbourne we moved into 46 Ardrie Road, just three houses away from our previous home. The house was almost identical in layout to No 40, so it felt very familiar. It had been a long journey and all three of us were really tired, Rodney especially. We had just settled him into bed, when Pat came across the street to invite us for a meal that evening. We accepted gratefully, and said we would be over as soon as Rodney woke up. After a few hours he was still sleeping, so one of Pat's girls came over to keep an eye on him, while we went for a lovely meal with the rest of the family. We returned home and Rodney was still sleeping. Eventually we had to wake him—he had slept for a full twenty-four hours, and we were worried that he would be dehydrated. He was soon back to his lively self again though, riding up and down the hallway on his little red plastic motorbike.

When Geoff returned to work he was welcomed with open arms. Lance, the Works Manager at *Crestknit* said, "Thank goodness you're back—get all those machines working!"

His workmates told him that half the machines in his section had been out of commission for weeks while he had been away. By the end of that first day Geoff, who was now a knitter and mechanic, had all the machines running smoothly. I returned to my part-time job too, much to Pat's relief, and we settled back into our daily routine.

Our priority now was to get a mortgage as soon as possible to secure our first home. The owner of the house on *Wilmot Street* had not put it up for sale, but was now anxious to sell up and move away, and we didn't want to lose the chance of buying it. This small bungalow was ideal for us—only a short walk along *Ardrie Road,* then through *Ardrie Park* to *Wilmot Street*, which is a short street leading onto *Dandenong Road*. It was close to our new friends too, and all the local amenities, with the suburb of *Carnegie* just on the other side of *Dandenong Road* over the railway line, with a good shopping centre.

We gave the owner of the house a small deposit to hold it for us, and then made an appointment with our bank. After an hour of discussing our past savings and future earnings, we were turned down for a loan. I was devastated, and so upset that all our hard work and planning had been in vain. After a few days of coming home to a distraught wife, Geoff suggested that we should make another appointment at the *State Bank of Victoria*, but this time with the manager. He went over our finances with us and said that the money we had recently spent on our overseas trip should have been taken into account, as it showed how much we were able to save previously. He agreed a mortgage for us of $17,000—with us paying $5,000 deposit to make up the asking price of $22,000.

We were thrilled, and couldn't wait for everything to be arranged so that we could move into our very first home. To help with expenses we also received a government grant of $700, which was given to first home buyers of properties up to the value of $22,000. We had worked out our incomings and outgoings, and knew we could manage well when, just a few months after taking out our mortgage with an interest rate of 7%, it shot up to 9%, which would make quite a difference to our monthly repayments. Fortunately, instead of increasing the amount, the bank changed the length of the mortgage from eighteen years to twenty-one, which was a huge relief.

Geoff, Rodney and I, with our budgie Charlie, moved into 18 *Wilmot Street* before Christmas and set out to make it a comfortable home. We had bought a two-seater sofa and footstool from the former owner for the open-plan kitchen, but we still needed a dining table and chairs.

We found a good, solid rectangular table and four chairs in a secondhand furniture shop on *Waverley Road*, and I spent hours sanding, staining and varnishing these while Geoff was at work. (It was the only time I did anything like this, but I was pleased with the result). Some time later we bought a slim 5' tall fridge/freezer for the kitchen—which seemed large to us, but was hardly average size to Australians. This was brought home to us on an outing with Pat and Fred to buy some fresh meat in bulk. Pat and Fred bought a whole lamb, which was butchered into joints at source. Geoff and I bought just half a lamb and struggled to get it into our fridge/freezer, but it was good value, and lasted us for many weeks.

Rodney loved our big back garden, with his tree house built into a dead tree at the bottom of the garden. This was low, with just three steps to climb into it, so quite safe. The above-ground round swimming pool was great for cooling off on hot days. It was 15' in diameter and about 4' high, with the water 2-3 feet deep, so he had to be supervised when playing in and around the pool.

We spent a lovely Christmas in our new home—I even cooked a traditional hot roast turkey dinner in the 90°F heat, and I then went to *Evancourt Hospital* in the afternoon for my 2-hour shift in the hot kitchen.

The new year (1974) was a very happy one for us, as we settled into this new phase of our life. In February we decided to have a barbecue, as a joint housewarming and celebration of Geoff's 29th birthday. We had bought a barbecue made up of concrete and stone slabs, which bolted together, and situated it next to the lemon tree. We invited our friends Pat, Fred and family, Jim, Dot and their children, Dave, Ann and Dave's brother and family, who had just arrived in Australia, Tony & Betty, and some of Geoff's workmates. The men busied themselves with cooking the steak and sausages on the 'barbie', while the ladies helped with the salads, and the children had a good time in the tree house and pool. We played our favourite music by *The Stones*, *The Beatles*, *Tom Jones*, *Credence Clearwater Revival* and *Abba*, who were becoming very popular in Australia at that time, and they went on to win the *Eurovision Song Contest* later that year. The residents of this quiet street must have wondered exactly who had moved into the neighbourhood!

It was difficult keeping up with the supply of cold beer for the men, and so Geoff filled our small freezer with bottles of *Victoria Bitter*, and then promptly forgot about them. After everyone had gone home he remembered, and when he opened the freezer door he found the bottles had exploded! We had quite a bit of clearing up to do after the party, especially the stones and beer bottle tops in the pool, and we made a decision to take it down, as we were worried that Rodney could now stretch up and reach the edge, and we didn't want any accidents. Geoff siphoned off the water and we collapsed the pool. We didn't really miss it, as we lived close to our local swimming pool, and to the city beaches, and we could always visit those on hot weekends and in the evenings.

Later that year we received a nice tax refund in the post, and decided to use it as a deposit on a new car. In Australia the tax year ends in June, and most workers spend that month filling in a multi-page document listing all tax paid, and the cost of visits to the doctor, dentist and pharmacy amongst other things, which are tax-deductible. It was a tedious task, but usually well worth the effort.

We looked at several makes of car, and Geoff decided on a *Honda Civic* 1260cc, a 2-door hatchback. This was a new model—so new in fact, that when we drove around the city and suburbs other people driving the same car would flash their lights. We had to order in advance and decided on the basic model with no frills. It came in several colours, and we said, "Any colour but orange." A few weeks later the salesman rang to say that he had a car available, and when Geoff asked the colour, he said, "Orange". We declined, and had to wait another couple of weeks for something we were happy to accept. This was in a shade of chocolate brown with gold flecks, which sparkled in the sunshine. We loved it, and it even had a radio—an optional extra. It was a lovely, well-made and reliable small car, and we were very happy with it.

We decided to try it out on a 3-day trip to *Mildura*, 542km (336 miles) north-east of Melbourne, situated on the *Murray River*. We packed a small, bright orange tent (with built-in ground sheet to keep out the spiders!) into the back of the car, with some sleeping bags and provisions and set off. We didn't have to drive too far out of the city before we saw some trees full of the native green budgerigars, and other trees that looked like white candyfloss from a distance, but were actually full of cockatoos, and as we approached they all flew off in a white cloud, then all turned together, revealing their pink undersides.

Mildura is a citrus fruit-growing region, and orange trees were growing close to the highway on both sides—we could have reached out to pluck them as we drove past. We bought a case of them to take back to Melbourne at a cost of about one cent each. Grapes are widely grown too, and there are many wineries in the area. We pitched our little orange tent in a clearing and explored our surroundings before settling down for the night. There was a thunderstorm that night with heavy rain, but we stayed cosy and dry in our tent. The next day we explored the area—and really enjoyed a trip on a paddlesteamer on the *Murray River*. After a second night sleeping in our cramped accommodation, Rodney said: "Do we live here now?" We could see how he was confused, with the frequent moves we had made in his first three years.

24

Wedding bells

We had an addition to our family this year too. Ray's dog, a Beagle, had a litter of puppies and we took Rodney to see them. They were cute little things—quite irresistible. Pat and Fred had adopted one of the pups, and called him Snoopy. Of course we couldn't go home empty-handed, and we took one little wriggling bundle back with us to *Wilmot Street*. We called him Mick.

Mick and Rodney on our front porch

Geoff's family had always had at least one dog in their home, and he grew up with them. I, on the other hand, remember there were mostly cats in our house when I was young, but then my sisters bought me a black Spaniel cross puppy for my 14th birthday. I called him Bruce. (I've no idea how I came up with that Aussie name). He was lovely, and like Geoff's family's dogs, was intelligent and easy to train, so we thought it would be no problem instilling discipline into our new arrival. We were wrong.

Mick, despite having a large garden to play in and lots of walks to the park at the end of the street, was never still. If I did any gardening, such as planting bulbs or putting in decorative edging to the borders, he would immediately dig them up. He chewed the plastic handlebars off Rodney's bike, and ate any small toys left around. He was very destructive and I think the final straw was when I had hung clean sheets out on the rotary clothes line to dry, only to look out of the kitchen window a few minutes later to see Mick hanging onto the bottom of one of the sheets as it swung round in the breeze, tearing the sheet in half. When he was a year old there was no improvement in his behaviour, and Geoff was tired of coming home from work to hear complaints of what he had been up to, so we made a decision to find him a new home. One of Geoff's workmates took him off our hands. He was now with other dogs and a larger family, which suited him better, and we could settle down to a quiet life again.

We went to our first Australian wedding this year—my ex-work colleague John married Gwyn in a hotel close to the sea. The service was conducted in the hotel, and then the bride and groom and all the guests crossed the road to have photographs taken on the beach, before returning to the hotel for the wedding reception. It was a lovely setting, not something that could be done in Britain at that time, as most weddings had to be in a church or registry office. Unfortunately not long after this lovely occasion John's mum, our friend Mrs Allen, died. It was quite sudden, and a shock to everyone who knew her. We were very sorry, as she was a lovely lady and had been very kind to us.

Another wedding we attended around that time was Julie's, Jim and Dot's eldest daughter. The couple were married in a restaurant in the *Dandenong Ranges*, a beautiful venue just an hour's drive from Melbourne, with views looking west to the city's skyline. The guests all surrounded the happy couple for the wedding service, and then sat at small tables for the wedding dinner, followed by dancing into the evening. The night-time views from what was then

Mount Dandenong Observatory were spectacular. The restaurant closed in 1997, but re-opened in 2004 after extensive renovations, and the name was changed to *SkyHigh Mount Dandenong*, making it a very popular tourist destination and wedding venue once again.

Also not to be missed in the *Dandenong Ranges* is the tranquil *William Ricketts Sanctuary*, a 4-acre block of land with *Ricketts'* clay sculptures of Aboriginal figures and Australian animals hidden amongst the ferns, rocks and native trees. *Ricketts* sold the land to the Victorian Government in the 1960s, but continued living and working there. He was in his nineties when he died there in 1993.

News from our family and friends in Leicester was always eagerly awaited. As is the custom in Australia, our postbox was mounted on the front garden fence, and I walked to it several times a day to check for any blue airletters. There was only one delivery a day, and none at the week-end. One day I opened the top of the metal box, and there was the biggest spider I had ever seen sitting on top of a letter from home. I slammed the lid shut and ran back to the house. I had to wait all day until Geoff came home from work, and even he couldn't believe the size of it (about 3" in diameter). He opened the lid, sprayed it with some insecticide, and quickly shut the lid again.

I had to wait for the spider's demise before he could dispose of the corpse and retrieve the special letter for me to read.

Parcels from family were exciting to receive too. Rodney was the best dressed little boy around, with clothes from *Mothercare* sent by his Aunt Pat, and shirts and cute dungarees from his Aunty Anne, who worked at *Wards, a clothing manufacturer* in *Bradgate Street,* Leicester.

The news wasn't always good. My sister Pat, wrote to say my mum wasn't well, and after replying, it was so hard to wait to hear how she was. It was especially hard to hear of the death of Geoff's grandfather (Josh), and to not be able to attend his funeral—but letters brought good news too. Roy and Barbara, our friends in *Perth*, wrote of the birth of their new baby Adam, and sent photos. Ted and Olive, who had returned to *Perth*, wrote about their baby son, and Dave and Anne also had a daughter. In Leicester Rod and Cassandra sent us news of the births of their two daughters, and sent lovely photos of them both. Jan, who I had worked with at *Kemptons*, had married Brian and they had a boy and girl while we were away. Of course some of our cousins on either side of our family were also marrying and having children too—quite a population explosion on both sides of the world!

We hadn't intended to increase our family again at this time—but Rodney had other ideas.

One Sunday we were returning from an afternoon drive, when we drove past an orchard farm, selling apples and apple juice at the roadside. We stopped to buy some, and Rodney went exploring. There was a box in the corner of a large barn, and Rodney trotted over to see what was making the squeaky noises. It contained a female black cat suckling five tiny kittens. The man selling the apples came over, plucked one out of the box and handed it to Rodney, saying, "You can have this one". Geoff shouted, "No!" but it was too late—Rodney squeezed it to his chest and said, "It's mine!". We returned home with a box of apples, some fruit juice and a cute black kitten. Rodney was wondering what to call it, and Geoff said, "Well it's a boy—a tom cat . . . .", so Rodney immediately said, "I'll call him Tom". He grew into a big, handsome all-black cat, and often left us gifts of little rodents on the back step. One day he left the carcass of a 'possum, in several large pieces.

Rodney in the garden with Tom

There were changes at my place of work towards the end of the year. Wynne, who I worked with at *Evancourt Hospital*, hadn't been too well, and so decided to retire. She also stopped working for Bill, our next-door neighbour, but we still kept in touch and I often walked over with Rodney to visit her in her small flat in *Carnegie*. The new cook/chef was a man who had previously run his own restaurant. He had retired, but said he wanted to earn some 'pocket money'. He was nice to work with, but he decided to completely change the menus. Instead of salmon fishcakes and scrambled eggs, he cooked pork chops and steak, but the elderly patients couldn't really cope with such solid food. I sometimes took the meals into the patients' rooms to help them eat, but most of them didn't have much appetite. While we still had Mick, I used to take the unwanted cooked steaks home for him—he certainly enjoyed them!

One day after Geoff had gone to work I was feeling quite ill, with pains in my chest when I breathed. I put Rodney in his pushchair and managed to walked round to *Waverley Road* to visit our new GP, Dr Steptoe. He listened to my chest, and said that I had 'flu, and that I should go home to rest in bed for a few days—not easy when your husband is at work and you have a lively toddler. I did as I was told though, and managed to get home and into bed. Rodney played with his toys, and I managed to get up to make him a quick jam sandwich and drink before collapsing back into bed. I didn't feel too ill, just weak. In the afternoon Rodney couldn't go out to play, so he sat on the bed playing music to me on his guitar—it was lovely, but we were both very glad when Geoff arrived home.

I didn't like letting the hospital down, but wasn't fit enough to go into work for a week. When I did return one of the nurses asked, "Is your cold better?"

25

Avon calling!

Rodney had started attending kindergarten (nursery) two mornings a week. There was a waiting list for places, so his pal Graeme, who had started earlier, went on different days. The first time I took him I wasn't sure what to expect, as he had never been left with strangers before. The staff were lovely though, and chatted to him before showing him the toys and games and introducing him to some of the other boys and girls. I was told I could stay as long as I wanted to make sure Rodney was settled, and to be reassured that he would be fine. I followed him at a distance when he went outside to play with the other children in the sandpit, and after a few minutes he turned to me and said, "You can go now." I felt really sad that my little boy was growing up so fast and didn't need me so much now. It was quite a distance to walk to the kindergarten on *Burke Road*, and by the time I had walked home and made myself a cup of tea, it was almost time to collect him. He'd had a great time and couldn't wait to go again. He always enjoyed his time there, and played well with the other children, though there was the occasional fight over a certain fireman's helmet. I think he was changing his mind about his future career, his first choice had been to be a tram driver.

The mothers of the children at the kindergarten took it in turns to stay and help with supervision and the preparation of fruit and drinks mid-morning. On one of the occasions I had stayed to help out, I was standing next to a small tree in the garden watching the fun and games, when a boy of three or four fell out of the tree and landed at my feet! My heart stopped for a few seconds, and then he jumped up and ran off to play, none the worse for his tumble—unlike me, who could imagine a quite different outcome.

Geoff and I had become friends with a young Australian couple living almost opposite us on *Wilmot Street*, David and Rosemary—Geoff being particularly interested in David's 1913 *Hotchkiss* fire engine. They had a boy Scott aged two, and he and Rodney enjoyed playing in each others gardens, while we mums chatted over coffee. Rosemary and I talked about having another baby, and we both decided that now was the time—we just had to get our husbands to agree! That was no problem, and I was soon pregnant, closely followed by Rosemary. Soon afterwards I walked to the pharmacy on *Waverley Road* and bought my baby-to-be a Snoopy soft toy.

As in my first pregnancy I kept very well, and was looking forward to the birth of our second child in December 1975. One morning when I was just three months pregnant, Rosemary came to the door with little Scott. Without any preamble she announced, "Scott has German measles." She was smiling and didn't seem at all concerned, even though she was also two months pregnant. Of course German measles (rubella) is a relatively mild illness, but can cause miscarriage or defects in babies whose mothers have been in contact with those with the disease and who may not be immune, and Scott had been in our house playing with Rodney only the day before.

Rosemary was surprised when I didn't invite them in, but I apologised and said that I needed to ring the doctor as soon as possible. Rodney was at kindergarten, so I walked to the telephone box and made an appointment with the doctor. He saw me straight away, and arranged for me to have a blood test at *Cabrini Hospital* that afternoon. I called into Pat's and she offered to give me a lift. We arranged for Rodney and Graeme to be minded by a neighbour, while Pat drove me to the hospital for the blood test. It was all done very quickly, and then all I had to do was wait for the result.

Over the next few days I called into the surgery twice to ask if they had heard anything, but both times the answer was "No." I was beginning to worry now, as I knew the choice I would be offered if there was a positive result— either to go ahead with the pregnancy and hope for the best, or have an abortion. On the tenth day I paid another visit and asked the receptionist if the hospital had contacted them yet. After she shook her head yet again I said, "Well, I'll wait here until you do hear from them." I sat down in the waiting room, determined not to move until I had my answer. This ploy worked, and within half-an-hour I was told that my result was negative. The relief was enormous, but I was very upset that I had been fobbed off for so long, when a simple telephone call was all that was required to put my mind at rest about something so important to me and my family.

I finished working at *Evancourt Hospital* quite early in my pregnancy, as I wasn't enjoying it as much now that my friend Wynne had left. This resulted in me having lots of time on my hands, and I decided to try making some of the food that Geoff was missing which his grandmother had given him often when he was growing up. The first delicacy I made from 'scratch' was faggots (meatballs). These are made with minced pigs liver (very messy), chopped pork shoulder, bacon, onions, breadcrumbs and parsley. I served them the good old-fashioned way with mashed potatoes, peas (not mushy!) and onion gravy. Geoff really enjoyed this traditional British food, but it was the only time I cooked them myself. He had to wait until they became available in the butcher's shop or the supermarket.

Quite foolishly I then decided to try another recipe from my British Cook Book—pork pie. I'm not a big fan myself but Geoff is, so I thought I'd give it a go. This, as the name applies, is based on pork again (sorry Sue!), with bacon and sage and thyme seasoning. The hardest part to make was the hot water pastry (with lard!). This solid 7" diameter pie took a couple of days to make—and was eaten in about the same time. I never made it again—I leave these things to the experts (at Melton Mowbray) now, and we have it mainly as a Christmas treat.

I was always pleased to see visitors—one of whom was an *Avon* representative. She called regularly, and I usually bought one or two cosmetics and some perfume from her. Over a cup of coffee one day she told me that she was moving away and wouldn't be calling again. She then surprised me by asking if I would like to take over! I laughed and explained to her that I was a few months pregnant, but she persuaded me by saying that I could work just the hours I wanted, and that it was a good way to meet new people.

So I was now an *Avon* 'lady'. It was true that it was a way to meet new people—mainly housewives who were at home during the day, and happy to chat for a few minutes. I didn't have a big round in the neighbourhood, and I think I bought more items myself than I sold, so it didn't earn me anything, but it was a fun part-time occupation and with all the perfumes I treated myself to, I always smelled nice!

Pat and I were still going to our slimming club meetings weekly, and it was when I was a few months pregnant that I was the 'slimmer of the week' after losing two pounds. (It must have been all that 'Avon calling'!) I don't think the group always took dieting seriously, but the meetings were good fun.

I was keeping well and getting plenty of exercise on my *Avon* round and walking Rodney to and from kindergarten, but summer was approaching, and I was feeling quite hot and bothered. My hair wasn't too long but I wanted a style that was easy to manage, and on impulse I booked myself an appointment at the hairdressers for a perm. I explained that I wanted a soft perm, just to give my hair some 'lift' and 'body', essentially an easy-to-manage style.

After two hours I left the salon with a head covered in tight curls, but with the assurances of the stylist that after a few days these would loosen into soft waves, and that a wash and blow dry would give the 'body' I was hoping for. I wasn't too sure, but hoped for the best, because the person looking back at me from the mirror was unrecognisable. This drastic change in appearance was confirmed when on the way home, having stopped to talk to a friend on *Ardrie Road*, Geoff drove past and despite my frantic waving, didn't know me, and so didn't pick me up. Years later, when looking at some old photographs from that time, our daughter told me that I looked like Ronald McDonald!

I have always loved Christmas, and really enjoy buying and wrapping presents. I found some great pyjamas for Rodney, kung fu style, with black trousers, a white wraparound top and a black belt. My favourites though were the ones we sent as presents to our nephews in England—convict style, with arrows printed all over them.

Rodney in his kung fu pyjamas

I was provisionally booked into *Cabrini Hospital* for my due date of 18th December but, like Rodney, this baby was not to be rushed. I was still continuing my stint as an *Avon* rep, sometimes accompanied by Rodney. My customers took a keen interest in my pregnancy, and one particularly hot summer day, at nine months pregnant and almost bursting out of my cotton maternity dress, my knock on the door was answered, and yet again I was asked, "Haven't you had that baby yet?"

26

A special gift

We had some good news from Leicester towards the end of 1975. My mum was retiring in December, and had booked her second trip to come to Australia in January 1976. All I had to do now was produce our new baby, who was showing no signs of making an appearance. As Christmas approached it was hard to make plans, with not knowing if any festivities would be interrupted by me going into labour. Dr Steptoe talked to me about the possibility of inducement. I was reluctant, but he said he would definitely want me in by Boxing Day, so we agreed I should go in earlier, and hopefully have my baby before Christmas Day itself.

So once again Geoff took me to *Cabrini Hospital* early on Christmas Eve morning—I hadn't wanted to stay at the hospital the night before on my own waiting for something to happen. Geoff had left Rodney to play with Scott so he didn't stay for long, and I walked about the maternity unit, chatting with the new mums while waiting for the medical interventions to take effect. Geoff returned later when I was well and truly in labour, and after a couple of hours he told me to "Hurry up." I was doing my best! He was anxious about leaving Rodney though and the staff sent him home, assuring him that it would be a while yet, and that he should ring to check on my progress in a few hours. The maternity unit at the hospital was very quiet at this time of year—obviously other mums had planned their pregnancies better than me. The nurses and nuns were really kind and attentive, and made me as comfortable as possible.

At 8pm on Christmas Eve Geoff rang the hospital again, and was told that he should come in, as it wouldn't be long now. He walked to Pat and Fred's with Rodney, and Fred offered to sit with him while Geoff came to the hospital. Geoff put Rodney to bed at home, and Fred sat watching television while Geoff drove to the hospital, hoping to be in time for our baby's arrival. Unfortunately, he still had a while to wait. Dr Steptoe was also summoned to the hospital—he had to leave a dinner dance, and arrived at the hospital in formal black tie. Things were not straightforward, with the threat of another forceps delivery, but this time they weren't needed, and our daughter was born at one minute past midnight on Christmas Day 1975, weighing 8lb 4.5oz. The midwife asked me what name we had chosen for a girl, then went out to Geoff and said, "You have a little Suzanne Patricia." We were both thrilled of course, and after Geoff had been in to see me and our new baby girl, he went home to share the good news with Fred, who was dozing in a chair. Fred congratulated him, and then went home to play Santa to his own five children.

Geoff slept for a few hours, and then had to wake Rodney later on Christmas morning to tell him that he had a baby sister. Rodney's response was to ask, "Has Santa been?" He was pleased to hear about the new baby, but at the time was much more interested in his new scooter, which had blow-up tyres and a footbrake. Geoff came for a brief visit to see his two girls in hospital before taking Rodney to Dot and Jim's house in *Ferntree Gully*, where they were to have Christmas lunch. Sadly, instead of a day full of Christmas cheer, they were met with a very strained atmosphere. Dot and Jim were of course pleased for us on hearing about our Christmas baby, but they weren't talking to one another. Dot told Geoff that there would be no Christmas dinner, as Jim had spent all the money on a new stereo sound system.

Rodney on his new scooter, Christmas Day 1975

They did all have a nice meal though, and Rodney enjoyed playing with their two boys, Richard and Martin, and showing off his new scooter, which Geoff had carried in the boot of the car. I, on the other hand, had a lovely Christmas lunch in hospital. I had recovered well from the birth, and around mid-day tucked into a delicious 4-course meal. I was in a small 2-bed room this time with a bathroom, and the sun was shining—the temperature outside was 102°F, but it was very pleasant in the air-conditioned room. The only disappointment was that the other mum was a smoker. She did have the bed next to the window and was considerate about when she smoked, but it's hard to believe now that it was allowed, especially in a room where babies came to be nursed. I was managing better with breastfeeding this time, so was very happy. That evening Geoff visited me, and then went to the nursery to see all the babies being held up in their small cradles to be admired from behind the glass screen. Someone asked, "Why is that baby's crib decorated in red ribbons and bows?" Geoff explained, "She's my daughter, and she is the Christmas baby." It was the custom for this Catholic hospital to do this to celebrate the first baby born on Christmas day.

I was in hospital for just seven days this time and had a few visitors, including Wynne, as well as Dot and Jim, who were friends again. Geoff sent off the telegrams to our families in Leicester, so my mum knew of our daughter's arrival before she set off on her long flight to see her Australian grandson and granddaughter. Geoff visited me every day, often leaving Rodney to play with Scott. It was very kind of Rosemary to look after him, and we were really cross with Rodney when we heard he'd had a falling out with his playmate and had hit him, especially as he was so much younger. Geoff made him apologise of course, and they remained friends. Rosemary had her baby a few weeks after me, a little brother for Scott.

Mum arrived on 4th January 1976, when Sue was just ten days old. We went to collect her from *Tullamarine* airport, and while we were waiting I took baby Sue to change her, while Geoff and Rodney waited to greet mum. It was another hot day, around 103°F, and Sue was in her carrycot wearing just a nappy and tiny lilac cotton top. Mum saw Geoff and Rodney first, and then was surprised to see me with our baby, as she thought I would still be in hospital. It was lovely to see her again, and to introduce her to her latest grandchild. Geoff picked up one of her suitcases and she said, "Wait 'til you see what's in there." It contained lots of pink clothes for our new baby girl—my sister Pat had been on a spending spree in *Mothercare*! Mum had bought presents for Rodney too. I think his favourite was something she had bought for him and Graeme—'snaky' belts. These were elasticated belts, with a metal buckle in an S-shape. Geoff had always worn one to keep his trousers up when he was a young lad, and it was nice to see they were still in fashion!

Rodney and Graeme in two of my knitted creations!

Mum loved her second holiday in the sunshine. She had a go at cooking meat on the barbecue, and gave Sue lots of cuddles in the shade of our fruit trees in the garden. She also took Sue for walks to give me a break. One particular day though she had been gone a long time, and I was getting anxious. She had become lost, and when she did find her way back, was very overheated and disoriented. As she was diabetic I was very concerned, but after a cool drink and a rest, she was fine.

We walked to the shops on *Waverley Road* daily, and often called into the local charity shop. In Australia they are called 'Opportunity Shops', but mum called them "Opportunity Knock Shops", mixing them up with a talent show on television in Britain at the time. One day we found a good sunhat for Rodney—it was a white canvas cap that came down over the eyes, with round, darkened plastic discs to see through. Mum tried it on outside the shop, and I couldn't stop laughing at how ridiculous she looked. She didn't mind, and I realised it had been a long time since I had laughed so much. I bought a lovely marcasite brooch from there too, in the shape of a kangaroo, for 50 cents.

Our friends Pat and Fred had a block of land on *Phillip Island*, with a small wooden holiday bungalow on it. They said we were welcome to use it, and so we planned a trip to show mum this lovely and very popular tourist spot. We had always wanted to return to see the 'Penguin Parade', so this was a perfect opportunity. All five of us squeezed into our car, along with all the paraphernalia essential for transporting a new baby, and Geoff drove the 87 miles on a hot, sunny day. Pat and Fred's block was in a lovely position, and we were very pleased to arrive in the early afternoon. Geoff parked the car, and then unlocked the door of the bungalow. It was dark inside and as he drew back the curtains at the windows, dozens of huge moths flew out into the room—why is everything so *big* in Australia? I stayed outside with Rodney and baby Sue, while Geoff and mum tried to shoo them out. We unpacked and then went off to have a look around the island. It was getting late, so we drove to the Nature Park and settled down on the stone steps built on the beach for visitors to rest and wait for the 'Penguin Parade' spectacle at sunset.

It was a long wait, but our patience was well rewarded, When it was almost dark, spotlights were shone out over the waves, and one by one the cute little creatures stood upright at the water's edge, and when a few had gathered together, they waddled up the beach, passing within inches of the onlookers, but intent on finding their own burrows to feed their hungry families. There are up to 70,000 Little (Fairy) Penguins on *Phillip Island*, and around 6,000 in the area of the 'Penguin Parade', and it takes one to two hours for all of the little groups to walk up the incline to their burrows. The penguins are just 12-13" (30-33cm) tall, with dark blue heads and flippers and white chests. As we walked back to the car we passed close to some of the penguins, but they stayed focussed on their task, determined to reach home to feed their young. It was a special experience, and Rodney loved these little creatures, but Sue slept through it all—it was many years later before she returned to Phillip Island to see them.

Little (Fairy) Penguins

We returned to our accommodation for the night hoping that the moths had dispersed, but many were still around, so after everyone was settled for the night, we put off the lights, but kept a candle burning in a far corner for the remaining moths to gather around the flame. I sat upright in a chair all night with Sue in my arms, not wanting to be asleep with creatures flying around my head—I'm such a coward!

The next morning Geoff had his own scary encounter. He went to use the outside toilet, and turning round saw the same type of spider that had been in our letter box—3" in diameter with long legs stretching across a wicker rake propped at the back of the toilet! He made a hasty retreat, and we all used the facilities at the nearest pub that morning.

We spent a few hours more exploring beautiful Phillip Island before returning home. It had been a lovely break, and mum had some great photos to show to family and friends on her return to Leicester.

27

Pain and suffering

One day when I collected Rodney from kinder, I saw he had been crying and he said that his shoulder hurt. The staff told me that he'd had an accident in the playground—another boy had pushed him when he was standing on a tyre. It was lying flat on the ground so he hadn't fallen far, but he had put out his hands to save himself and had landed awkwardly. The pain was in the area of his collarbone, but the staff didn't think he had broken it. I acted on their advice though and took Rodney straight to our GP surgery. The doctor arranged for him to go to *Cabrini Hospital* for an x-ray. Luckily I was able to leave Sue with mum while I took him for this, which did confirm he had a simple fracture of his right collarbone. Of course there is no treatment, other than to put the arm in a sling for several weeks, and to keep it as immobile as possible. Fortunately it was the middle of summer, so Rodney didn't need to struggle in and out of his clothes—he mostly wore just shorts and a sling for his arm. He couldn't go back to kinder though for a few weeks, or ride his scooter, but otherwise he coped very well. Sue loved having her big brother at home with her all the time—she would cry when he wanted to go out to play with his friends.

Sue and Rodney in the garden

Geoff decided to grow some vegetables in the long, hot summer and started with some butternut pumpkins (squash). These just grew and grew with very little effort on Geoff's part, spreading all over the small vegetable patch, just requiring plenty of water. We had squash with every meal for weeks—it was especially nice mashed up with potato.

His other successful crop was tomatoes, which flourished in the outdoors—just needing copious amounts of water and one other special addition to the soil. Fred kept some chickens (chooks) in his back garden, and had a surplus of chicken manure. He told Geoff he could have as much as he needed, so Geoff shovelled up enough of this foul-smelling (!) mixture to fill a wheelbarrow, walked with it from *Ardrie Road* to *Wilmot Street* and spread it over the vegetable patch. The resulting big red tomatoes tasted delicious—so delicious in fact that Geoff came out in a rash all over his face and chest after eating too many!

Fred's chickens quite often escaped from his back garden, and one day when he was rescuing one from a tree in *Ardrie Road*, an eccentric middle-aged lady, who lived a few houses away, shouted at him that it was cruel to keep chickens cooped up. (She was one to talk, as she kept her cats on long chains attached to the washing line in the back garden, so that they could run up and down, but not run free). Fred, who was half-way up the tree at the time, told her to "Sod off"—or words to that effect!

My mum, who had only planned to stay with us for two months, decided to stay longer, rather than go back to an English winter, which we were all pleased about—Rodney loved having his granny around, and baby Sue was just getting to know her. We took her to the immigration office and they were happy to stamp her passport to extend her visa for another month. This turned out to be a very fortunate decision for our small family.

In March one of Geoff's friends invited us to his engagement party, but we declined as we didn't want to leave mum to look after Rodney and Sue on her own. It was a Saturday, and in the afternoon, when Geoff was playing in the garden with Rodney, and mum and Sue were having an afternoon nap, I decided to take the chance to catch up on some gardening. We had yellow roses climbing up a fence at the side of the house alongside the kitchen window, and they needed pruning. I'm no expert, but I thought I could tackle this, so arming myself with a pair of secateurs and a chair, I started work.

The roses were well established and had thick branches, which were held against the fence with heavy wire netting. I snipped away at the dead roses, and was quite pleased with my efforts, pushing any stray branches behind the wire. One particular branch was hard to secure, but I thought I had managed to do it. I reached out to the right to snip off a dead flower and the branch shot back, hitting me forcefully in the left eye. I didn't fall off the chair, but managed to cling to the side of the house and get down safely. The pain was intense, and I could imagine myself with a big black eye the next day. I had no idea that there might be any damage to the eye itself. On Sunday I still couldn't open my eye and it was very painful. When it was the same on Monday I left mum to babysit, and walked to the telephone box to ring Dr Steptoe. He came to visit soon afterwards, and was very concerned about my eye. He said I should go to hospital immediately to have it checked. As Geoff was at work, Pat gave me a lift to the hospital, and after the consultant examined my eye he said, "I want you to go home and pack your pyjamas." Examination had revealed that a thorn had pierced my cornea, and I needed urgent treatment.

It was a shock, but I was in such pain that I would have agreed to anything. Pat dropped me at home, where I put a few things into a suitcase and waited for Geoff to get home from work. We then left mum to take care of Rodney and Sue while Geoff drove me to *Cabrini Hospital*. It was 22nd March, and Sue was less than three months old. I was still breastfeeding her, but fortunately had been supplementing her feeds with *Carnation* milk formula, so Geoff and mum could make up bottle feeds for her while I was away. I was kept in hospital for two nights, and treated with antibiotics to prevent infection. Mr Galbraith, the consultant said, "You have been lucky—if there had been any infection I would have had to remove your eye." Sue was due for a check-up the day I was admitted to hospital, and mum went to the clinic with Geoff to get her weighed and measured. When Geoff told the clinic nurse about my accident she was very sympathetic, and she called in to see me the next day before my discharge. As I was laying flat and had both eyes covered, she had to explain who she was!

I went home after the two days, but Mr Galbraith arranged a date for me to return to have the damaged lens in my left eye removed. I was still in a lot of pain, but managed to cope with mum's help. Unfortunately her holiday was coming to an end, and we took her to the airport at the beginning of April after her three months stay and sadly waved goodbye.

I went back into *Cabrini Hospital* a couple of weeks later for my operation. This was done under a general anaesthetic, and I stayed in hospital for a few days. Geoff bought Rodney and Sue in to see me, but my baby didn't know me, and it was upsetting being away from them all. I was given pain relief, but was very depressed. At home again I was still in a lot of pain and had double vision, with only being able to see light and shapes with my left eye. I wore a patch over this eye for a while, but it was very uncomfortable, so soon discarded it. At that time damaged lenses were not replaced routinely. I had to wait three months for my eye to heal before I could try wearing a contact lens. I was in pain for most of this time, even with the medication I was taking, and I remember one particular evening when it became almost too much. I was having a bath after the children were in bed and Geoff was watching television, and I remember thinking how easy it would be to slip under the water, when Geoff tapped on the bathroom door and said, "We've won on the lottery!" It made me sit up, and then he said, "We've won $10 (£5)." This made me laugh—for a few seconds I had imagined us living in the lap of luxury, but it did the trick and brought me back to reality, and to realise how silly I was being.

My first appointment to be fitted with a soft contact lens was quite successful, and it gave me reasonable sight. I returned home with a huge bag of equipment—a round electric boiler to sterilise the lens in every day, a saline drip to rinse the lens each time I removed it, and solution to put in the eye along with the lens. I didn't get on with the soft lens for long though, and tried a hard lens, but this had to be worn for a short time each day and then for longer periods and I was still having problems, so I gave up, and for several years managed to cope with the good vision in my right eye and the very limited vision I had in the left eye. Spectacles weren't really an option, as I would still have double vision.

Later that year I took Pat's four girls to see the film 'Gone with the Wind', made in 1939 and starring Vivien Leigh and Clark Gable, leaving Geoff to babysit. Even though my sight wasn't brilliant I loved it, and couldn't believe it was thirty-seven years old and I had never seen it before! I have since bought video and DVD copies, and whenever I have four hours to spare, I like nothing better than to settle down with tea and biscuits— or wine and chocolates—to enjoy it all over again, preferably on my own.

This year of 1976 still had some medical problems in store for us. After Rodney came home from kindergarten one day he said, "Look at the spots on my tummy." Of course, it was chicken pox! He had to stay at home because it is an infectious disease, and unfortunately he passed it on to his little sister. Rodney only had those few spots and was otherwise well, but poor Sue was covered in spots and was quite poorly. She wasn't yet a year old, and all we could do for her was to cover her in calamine lotion to cool her skin and help with the itching. I was really worried about her so I moved her cot into our bedroom with me, and sent Geoff to share with Rodney. Perhaps this wasn't such a good move because a week later Geoff answered the door to our friend Pat and he was scratching his head. She laughed and said, "Chicken pox!" Geoff didn't believe her, but the very next day he discovered she was right, as spots were appearing all over his body. We went through a lot of calamine lotion in the next few weeks! I seemed to be immune, so must have had chicken pox when I was young, though my mum never seemed to remember what we had suffered from when I asked her—I think with three young girls we probably had everything that was going around at the time. When Geoff was able to return to work he looked awful, with his face covered in scabs and unshaven—I'm surprised they even let him in the door!

By now we were quite glad that 1976 was coming to an end, though we did still have Christmas to look forward to, and Sue's first birthday on Christmas Day. Like her big brother at that age, she was already walking, and she loved riding on Rodney's little plastic bike, and in his yellow peddle car. We bought her a ride-on pony, which became a favourite toy, and she loved picture books. Granny Green sent her a doll nearly as tall as her, and she had lots of presents from our families. Of course, as it was Christmas too, Santa came, and there were many presents for us all under the tree. It was a lovely ending to a difficult year, and we hoped the new year would bring better times for us all.

Sue on Rodney's bike, November 1976

Sue 'reading', December 1976

28

Difficult decisions

The year of 1977 started very well, with a lovely trip to join Pat, Fred and family in *Anglesea*. This popular tourist spot is on the *Great Ocean Road*, 110km (68miles) southwest of Melbourne. It is a great place for families to fish, swim and surf. It also has a golf course where kangaroos graze on the fairways. We all especially enjoyed the pedalos on the water, except for Fred, who was recovering from a knee operation.

We also had a trip to *Hanging Rock*, a recreational reserve in the *Macedon Ranges*, 70km (43 miles) north-west of Melbourne. Our friend Wynne came with us, and we packed a picnic lunch to be enjoyed by the creek. *Mount Macedon* is a former volcano, and *Hanging Rock* is a geological formation created by activity over millions of years. It was named after a rock formation—a boulder suspended between others over the main pathway. This is a former Aboriginal dwelling place, used for initiations and ceremonies, and a reputed home of bushrangers. Horse races have been held at *Hanging Rock* for over one hundred years, and today it is a popular spot for rock climbers, with its many caves, tunnels and overhanging boulders.

Geoff took Rodney with him on the steady upward climb to see the long-ranging views over flat plains and farmland, and the distant forests of the *Macedon* and *Cobaw* ranges, while Wynne, Sue and I rested by the side of the creek. They had reached a high viewing area where, Geoff told us later, it became deathly quiet with no-one else around and not even a sound from the flocks of birds he had seen earlier. Geoff found it quite unnerving, so picked up Rodney and made a quick descent.

We enjoyed our picnic and the flora and fauna in the area, and returned home in the early evening. It wasn't until Geoff returned to work and talked about his eerie experience that he heard about the novel written in 1967 by Joan Lindsay called 'Picnic at Hanging Rock'. This story told of a group of schoolgirls and their teacher who, on Valentine's Day 1901, visited the site and disappeared, never to be seen again. This novel was made into a film of the same name in 1975, which we didn't see until our return to England, but Geoff could fully understand the inspiration for the book after experiencing the unsettling atmosphere at *Hanging Rock* himself.

At the beginning of February Rodney started his first term at *Lloyd Street School* on the other side of *Waverley Road*. His friends from *Ardrie Road* began at the same time, but were all in different classes. Rodney looked very smart in his short-sleeved grey shirt and grey shorts sent by family from *Mothercare*, and a green v-neck jumper which I had knitted, though he didn't really need this in the first weeks of an Australian autumn. He was five-and-a-half years old and already reading, but his teacher didn't give her new pupils books for the first fews weeks for some reason, although teachers in other classes for this age group did. Rodney found this very frustrating, as we did, but he quickly picked up other skills, such as how to count to ten in Greek! (There was quite a mixture of nationalities in the area).

He really enjoyed school, and we walked the short distance through *Ardrie Park* and across *Waverley Road* with other children and their mums. One little girl, Shae, was taken to school by her grandmother who lived a few houses away on *Wilmot Street*. Rodney and I called for them as we passed the house, and Shae stayed close to Rodney all the way to school. One day he complained to Geoff that she wouldn't leave him alone and kept trying to kiss him. Geoff told him not to worry—one day he would feel differently about girls!

There was a School Crossing Supervisor (Lollipop man) based on *Waverley Road* in the mornings and afternoons to see the children safely across the road. One tragic day a little girl of five or six, who had been holding the Crossing Supervisor's hand at the side of the road while he was waiting for a suitable time to stop the traffic, pulled her hand away and ran into the road, directly into the path of a car. She was killed instantly. It was such a shocking, unbelievable accident and no-one could imagine the pain and suffering of her family, nor the shock and guilt felt by the Supervisor, though he couldn't possibly be blamed for such an unexpected and tragic event. He never returned to work however.

Around this time Geoff's work was altering quite dramatically after a change of government and soaring inflation. A flood of imported cheap textiles from far eastern countries had severely damaged the Australian textile industry. *Crestknit* was taken over by a Taiwanese company in 1977, with fabric being imported from Taiwan instead of being made in Australia, and partly made up garments were also brought into the country. These were then finished off in Australian factories by attaching collars and cuffs, and then the whole garment labelled as 'Made in Australia'. It was not the work that Geoff enjoyed, and although he was still busy maintaining the machines and he was never on short time, he didn't enjoy his job as he had done over the last eight years, and thought of looking elsewhere for employment.

We had been talking about returning to England for a while and maybe buying our own business, so Geoff's dissatisfaction with work was one of the reasons we began to seriously consider doing so. I was also lonely a lot of the time and had begun to worry about things like what would become of Rodney and Sue if anything happened to the two of us—unlikely, but still a concern. We knew that our good friends in Australia would care for them initially, but of course they would have to return to England to family eventually, which would be traumatic for them. I also couldn't get used to Christmas in the heat—I really missed the traditional Christmases I had experienced growing up—lots of hot food, cold weather and cosy fires. We were both very keen too on trying our hand at running a newsagents in England as my cousins Iris and Jean were doing, so we made up our minds to go ahead. Once this joint decision had been made we began to make plans for another big change in our lives, hopefully one which would suit us and our two young children.

The first thing we did was to contact an estate agent to put our house on the market. Property prices had been rising steadily and we were hoping for a decent profit after settling our mortgage, to cover our travel costs and to give us a good deposit for a home and hopefully a business in England. The agent was optimistic and said we should have no problem selling our house, which was in a popular inner suburb of Melbourne. They suggested selling by auction and we agreed, so this was arranged for a few weeks ahead, giving time for photographs, advertising and paperwork to be completed.

House auctions in Australia are conducted on the property, usually at the front of the house in the garden if there is one, or on the sidewalk in the street, with prospective buyers and interested onlookers often spreading out into the road. Our auction was on a lovely sunny Saturday and drew quite a crowd, but unfortunately no buyer. The agent suggested more advertising and perhaps a drop in price, but we thought an 'open house' over a week-end might be a good idea. The firm didn't undertake these at week-ends though as they were busy with auctions, so we offered to do it ourselves. Our agent agreed and we arranged this for the very next week-end.

The next few days while Geoff was working I gave the house a spring-clean in preparation for the hordes of prospective buyers we were sure would be visiting. It was indeed a busy two days—we had up to a hundred visitors over Saturday and Sunday, mainly young people, but it was hard to know who were genuine house-hunters and who were just curious to see the inside of our small home. We had 'open house' on both days from 10am to 4pm, so had to keep everywhere clean and tidy for the many people coming through the front door, having a peep into every room, then congregating in the back garden for a chat. I couldn't prepare or cook any food during these hours to make a mess of the kitchen, except for small snacks for the children, and we were so pleased to be able to close the door at 4pm each day to relax and eat and drink. All the effort was worth it though, as we had a good offer for the house the next week, which we accepted. The buyers were a young married couple who we were sure would be as happy as we had been in this home and neighbourhood.

The next step was to contact a solicitor to deal with the legal and monetary details. We made an appointment expecting things to be quite straightforward, but were shocked when we were told that there was a caveat on the property— meaning we could not sell without permission from another source. We had completely forgotten that we had agreed to be guarantors for our friends Dot and Jim when they had taken out an extra home loan on their house in *Ferntree Gully*. They'd had a difficult time, losing their land in *Chirnside Park* because they couldn't keep up the payments, later having their car repossessed, and were now in danger of losing their home, so we agreed. I suppose we should have realised that this was a risk as even Dot's sister, who had recently arrived in Australia and was also living in *Ferntree Gully*, had refused to help. Dot and Jim were good friends though, and we didn't want to see them homeless.

It was an anxious time waiting to hear from our solicitor, but within a few days he rang to say that the loan company had agreed to waive the restriction as they had Geoff's contact details in England. It was such a relief as we'd had no idea of this injunction on our own property. In fact, soon after we had returned to England—even before our money from the sale of our house had come through (we lost out again financially with the devaluation of the Australian dollar this time)—the loan company was trying to contact us because Jim and Dot were not keeping up the repayments on their loan. Jim had set up his own business fitting aluminium cladding to weatherboard houses, and had filed for bankruptcy. Unbelievably, Dot had come to England for a holiday at the same time. We met up with her and she was unconcerned, thinking she could ignore any debts, but Geoff and I would certainly have had to honour our agreement. We contacted the loan company and asked them to write to us via our solicitors. We didn't hear from them, but it was a worry, as Geoff still had to find work to support us before we decided where in England we wanted to buy a business.

We realised much later that if we had changed our minds and decided to stay in Australia, we would have been responsible for repaying the loan ourselves, amounting to many thousands of dollars, perhaps even losing our own house in the process.

Meanwhile in Australia we could now go ahead with planning another big move—this time from Australia to England, and with two children in tow. We also had a houseful of furniture and a car to sell. Once the date for the handover of the keys to the house was arranged, we had just weeks to organise everything, including a flight to take all four of us back to England, a place we had always called 'home'.

29

Return journey

Before settling down to the serious business of organising our return to England, we took Rodney and Sue on a fun day out to *Kryal Castle*—a replica medieval castle located 8km east of *Ballarat*, which has a moat, drawbridge and maze amongst its many attractions. It was built in 1972 and opened to the public in 1974. The children really enjoyed seeing the jousting knights in the arena and the actors walking around dressed as lords and ladies in period costume. Of course Rodney and Geoff had to try out the wooden stocks, but sadly there was no rotten fruit around to recreate the original experience! I bought a lovely glass pendant for myself which has flakes of gold (maybe from the nearby gold fields of Ballarat) floating in liquid. This castle was a popular attraction at the time but went into decline. Happily, after extensive renovations it is now a thriving theme park and conference and wedding venue.

Now came the difficult problem of sorting out our belongings. We not only had the furniture, car and children's toys to sell, but also had to make arrangements for our pets. Friends came to the rescue once again, with Jim and Dot offering to adopt our budgie Charlie, which we accepted gratefully. We were more concerned about our cat, Tom, as cats are notorious for being more attached to their homes than their owners. We contacted the couple buying our house and they said that they would be happy to take over his care. It was so good of them, and was a huge relief to us. They also bought our fridge/freezer which was very convenient, as we were able to use it right up until we left.

The first item to be sold was a Victorian solid wooden two-seater school desk, which we had bought for Rodney. His little friend Shae had this, which we were pleased about. The only pieces of furniture we wanted to take back to England with us were a coffee table and side table. The tops of these wooden tables were made of fossilised slices of root from the mallee tree—a species of eucalyptus native to Western Australia. These had lovely colours, and we thought they would be a special reminder of our time in Australia. The coffee table measured 22" x 43" and Geoff had to make a packing case big enough to contain this. We had three standard size boxes too, and sorted out essential items we couldn't leave behind, such as favourite toys, some bedding, photo albums and most importantly, Rodney's *Tommy Turtle*—a plastic stepstool he stood on to use the toilet.

One by one our household and garden items were sold. Our mower was bought by a workmate of Geoff's who had just bought her first home, and our dining table and chairs which I had lovingly restored, found a new home with Flo and Ray. Fortunately we had an 'island bar' in the kitchen with a couple of high chairs which we could use for mealtimes in the interim. Gradually our home was being cleared, and Pat and Fred helped by loaning items to us to temporarily replace them. Our television was very old and we had lost the sound just before we were due to leave. Our neighbour Bill had one with no picture, so we gave him ours and he put one on top of the other to make a complete set! We borrowed Pat and Fred's small portable colour t.v.—the first one we had seen. They also lent us some bean bags after we sold our two sofas, which were very comfortable to sit in, but hard to get out of!

Eventually we had to put our beloved Honda car up for sale. We advertised it in the local newspaper and soon had a buyer. The car was three years old and in good condition, and we were really pleased to sell it for the same price we had paid for it—a result of the high inflation at the time. The buyer—a smart-looking man—told us that he was an airline pilot, and he wanted it to drive to and from the airport as he didn't like to leave his Jaguar in the car park when he was away—not sure we believed that!

During this time my cousin Iris had been sending us copies of the *Dalton's Weekly* newspaper, which contained details of many businesses for sale. It was exciting to read all about these, especially the newsagents, and to imagine being our own bosses. We knew it would be hard work, but perhaps didn't realise just how hard.

Rodney had a small party at home for his sixth birthday in July, and finished school a week later. His friends had been telling him that England was a very small country compared to Australia, and he wasn't sure what to expect. Little Sue was too young at twenty months to know what all the excitement was about, and was just happy to be wherever we were.

We had said good-bye to Flo, Ray and family and Flo gave us two special *Rosebud* spoons, one of which we are still using. Pat gave the children some books about *Blinky Bill* the koala, and we reluctantly said a last good-bye to our good friends.

Finally at the end of July 1977 we left our Australian home, leaving the keys with Bill for the new owners, and headed to the airport in a taxi to catch our *Qantas* flight to London, England. After nine years and seven months we were returning to Leicester to be reunited with family and friends we hadn't seen for so long. We were sad to be leaving Australia and the friends who had been such a big part of our lives, but were excited to be returning to familiar surroundings, and were looking forward to catching up with events that we had missed over the last few years.

Our flight to *Heathrow Airport* in London was long but uneventful, with a short break in *Singapore*. It was Sue's first flight and as she was so young we were given seats at the front of economy class with extra leg room, which was much more comfortable. After around twenty-five hours we were finally reaching the end of our journey. As we flew low over England for our landing, Rodney looked out of the window on the left of the plane, then ran to the right side to see the patchwork quilt of fields below and said, "England doesn't look that small to me."

The Qantas 747 at last touched down on the tarmac, and we walked through immigration to the baggage collection area. We found all our suitcases but one. Eventually the carousel was empty with no sign of our missing case. I went off to change Sue into a pretty summer dress while Geoff searched for it. He became impatient and climbed over the carousel, finding our lost case hidden behind a pillar where it had fallen. With

Sue now perched on top of our luggage on a trolley we emerged into the arrivals lounge, where our anxious families were waiting. It was a lovely warm welcome, and Sue met her aunts, uncles and cousins for the first time.

All that was left now to complete the circle of our journey around the world was to travel the relatively short distance from *Heathrow* in London to Leicester in the Midlands. This journey back to our roots however was not to be straightforward. The 100 miles, mostly on the M1 motorway, was to take almost as long as the 12,000 miles we had travelled from Australia, but that's another story . . . .

Sue, M1 Motorway, 1st August 1977

Epilogue

Emigration to Australia today is quite a different experience to that of nearly fifty years ago, when Geoff and I made our long journey to the other side of the world. There is no longer a '£10 Pom' scheme, and migrants have to pay their own travel expenses, unless sponsored by an employer. There are also restrictions on age and work experience—and only applicants with skills in demand in Australia are encouraged to apply.

The decision to emigrate has been made much easier by the arrival of the internet—employment, housing and education can be researched in detail before a final decision to emigrate is made. It is still a huge decision though to travel 12,000 miles to a new country, leaving behind family and friends, and a large percentage return within a few months or years.

In our case, after returning to England in 1977, we did miss Australia and thought of returning, but it was not to be. However our Australian-born children did return as adults. Rodney married in 1999 and he and his wife went to live in Melbourne. Sadly their marriage broke down, and Rodney returned to England in 2002. Sue, who obtained a degree at Sheffield University, went out in 2000 to undertake a Masters degree at

Melbourne University. She met her future husband there, and they now live in Melbourne.

We have learnt that wherever you are in the world life is unpredictable, and unfortunately along with the good times, there are usually some bad. We think fondly of our years in Australia because our children were born there in 1971 and 1975. Tragically we lost our son in a road traffic accident here in England in 2006.

We have never regretted our years living in Australia, and writing this book has brought back many happy memories of the places we visited and the people we met. We will never forget the kindness and generosity shown to us by our new friends, and I hope this book will demonstrate to them how much we appreciated it then and during the visits we have made since. We hope to see you all again soon!